Be

How I Survived My First Ten Years in the Classroom

By Franchesca Warren

The Educator's Room

Atlanta

Copyright @ 2013 The Educator's Room, LLC

All rights reserved.

www.TheEducatorsRoom.com

All rights reserved.

www.TheEducatorsRoom.com

The Educator's Room, LLC

P.O. Box 311770, Atlanta, GA 31131

Printed in the United States of America

ISBN: 978-0615852225

DEDICATION

This book is dedicated to all of teachers who needed help—this book is for you.

To my children, I love you more than there are words. Continue to strive for excellence.

To my husband, you are my rock. I love you.

To my siblings and my nieces, I told you I wasn't bossy—I just had leadership skills.

To my mother, you are my example of what it means to be strong and to depend on no one but myself.

To my father, because of you I delved into entrepreneurship. Thank you.

Contents

	Foreword by Michelle Armstrong	6
	Introduction	9
1	And Then I Was A Teacher	12
2	My Breaking Point	18
3	So You Got The Job—So What?	28
4	The Community Is Your School	33
5	Veteran Teachers Are Not The Enemy	46
6	Don't Break The Budget	54
7	Assumptions: How Many Of Us Have Them?	62
8	Professionalism 101	68
9	Lesson Plans: Don't Reinvent the Wheel	76
10	So You Have Started Teaching—What's Next?	82
11	It's Normal To Be Overwhelmed	88
12	Be the Boss of Your Classroom	94
13	It's Okay To Laugh, Right?	104
14	Communication Is A Necessary Evil	110
15	Do Your Job!	118
16	They Won't Leave My Room!	124
17	When Bad Things Happen To Kids	130
18	How To Create Your Own Professional Development	134
19	You Are A Brand—Act Like It!	138

20	Keep Your Resume Updated	146
21	If You Don't Want To Teach Until Retirement	150
22	Joy Comes In The End	154
	Afterword by Rhonda Black	157
	About the Author	159

Foreword

By Michelle Armstrong

When I began teaching in the late 1990s, I discovered I had a unique power to move students years beyond where they were academically when they entered my classroom. I had research to back me up. In the Education Trust's 1996 report, "The Real Value of Teachers," the researchers assert that "teacher effectiveness is the single biggest factor influencing gains in student achievement—not race, poverty, or parent's education."

Fast-forward almost 20 years later, and the same impact of teacher effectiveness is still echoes in countless policy and practice briefs throughout the field of education.

In recent years, especially with the federal government's Race to the Top initiative and the huge philanthropic support for education reform, a teacher's impact is still the largest factor in student achievement. The overhaul that many states have made (even in the teacher evaluation process) is largely due to what we have known since the days of one-room schoolhouses when blended, inclusive, multi-age classes were the norm. Teachers mattered then, and they matter now.

Given the span of my career as a teacher, a high school principal, and now teacher and principal effectiveness framework developer, Franchesca Warren presents pearls of wisdom for every new teacher entering his or her first years of teaching. As colleagues during a few of Warren's early years, I had the great privilege to witness her develop some of the very lessons that she shares in *Behind the Desk*. The practical, yet poignant tips for the trade that she presents are about more than surviving as a teacher; they are about *succeeding* as a teacher.

Many teachers entering the profession are facing more rigorous standards than ever. The field is abuzz regarding the types of instructional shifts that all educators will have to make to meet the demands of the forthcoming Common Core State Standards assessments. All teachers, especially new teachers, can benefit from the guidance that Warren brings. More than anything, I think *Behind the Desk* readers will have a better understanding of the stick-to-it-ness that it takes to become, not just good at teaching, but to become *great* at teaching!

For those who may pick up *Behind the Desk* after years of teaching, you will still find something meaningful. Warren's challenge to "brand yourself" is hugely important for teachers who love what they do and really want to evolve into better teacher-leaders.

With the recent introduction of the Teacher Leadership Exploratory Consortium's National Teacher Leader Model Standards, Warren gives thoughtful advice about how to hone related skills into other peripheral areas within the teaching profession. Warren's suggestions have the potential to not only enrich one's personal craft and pedagogy, but may also help other teachers improve, the school thrive, and all students grow to reach their highest potential. The lessons that Warren teaches from "behind her desk" are ones that will truly make in difference in the professional lives of teachers everywhere!

Michelle Armstrong is a Managing Director with Insight Education Group. She leads Insight's work in the states of California and Tennessee, including initiatives related to principal evaluation, teacher effectiveness and Common Core implementation.

Michelle holds a Masters degree in Education with an emphasis in Teaching and Curriculum from the Harvard Graduate School of Education and an undergraduate degree from Emory University. Additionally, Michelle is a past cohort member of New Leaders, a nationally recognized school leadership training residency, and has mentored aspiring school leaders through the program.

Introduction

I never knew I was going to be a teacher. I was supposed to graduate from college, become an attorney, and make a lot of money. But sometimes life goes into a different direction at the drop of a dime.

When I entered education, it was pretty calm. Districts were hiring, teachers were receiving raises, and unions were able to effectively bargain for us.

Then in 2008, everything changed. Districts stopped hiring as many teachers and increased class sizes. School budgets faced drastic cuts across the country. Teachers were laid off. As I watched all the developments, I noticed that new teachers suffered the most. Funds for professional development were nonexistent and I saw new teachers—with so much potential—leave the profession. After working with teachers around the nation, I realized I needed to use my skills that I had honed as a veteran teacher, to help my fellow teachers who were in their first five years of teaching.

This book started four years ago as a vision to give teachers real strategies not manufactured in a college classroom, but instead are tried-and-true methods that I have used in my 13 years of education. My proof is my students' success and the sense of calm I developed after learning systems that worked for everyone in my classroom.

I did not write this book to make outsiders feel better about teachers. Instead, I wanted to be honest about what I struggled with as a new teacher and how I handled it.

This book is for teachers—no one else.

I couldn't breathe.

There I was sitting frozen in my car trying to process how in exactly one hour I would be able to educate 16- and 17-year-olds looking to me for guidance. I had just graduated from college the year before and now here I was, about to teach in one of the largest urban districts in the state.

I was petrified.

Six months prior, I had decided to use my degree to teach high school English despite other professional offers. In the end, I had received offers to teach at two high schools within the city limits, but I struggled to see which one I'd "fit" in. I knew nothing about the school system, so I decided to ask several friends who were graduates from those schools. Amused by my dilemma, they looked at me and simply said, "You're not ready."

Using my gut instinct, I chose a school and signed my contract.

I was going to be a teacher.

1

And Then I Was A Teacher

I received my first teaching assignment in August 2003 at a small, urban school in downtown Memphis, Tennessee. From the time I signed the contract (April) until the time school started (August), I had roughly four months to get myself ready to be in the classroom.

I envisioned what teaching would be like. I reminisced on my time in high school and assumed that this school would not be much different. *Surely, teaching cannot be that hard*, I thought. Boy was I about to be wrong!

The next four months passed quickly. Before I knew it, I was headed to the district-mandated new teacher orientation. I thought I was going to learn all I needed to know (in those six hours) to be a "good" teacher. I envisioned an orientation where I got so much information that I wanted to be in the classroom the very next day. As I drove up to the location of orientation (a large high school in the city), I was immediately intimidated not only by the size of the school but also by the enormity of my job. Teachers change lives. Was I ready for that?

Six and half hours later, I walked out of the building with tons of paperwork about retirement contributions, direct deposit, my local union, and insurance—but no information about teaching.

I was confused. What was so important about orientation if nothing about actual teaching and learning was addressed? Was I going to find out about my job when I got to my school? Confused, I fell asleep by reassuring myself that I was going to make a difference in a child's life.

That following Monday morning, I reported to my new school and was quickly thrown into the trenches. There was no time for asking questions. I received the keys to my room and my schedules. I met fellow teachers and was introduced to my mentors. Before I knew it, Friday was here. School was starting in less than 72 hours. Even though the students were on their way, I didn't feel ready. On that Monday morning, I kissed my family goodbye and drove to my first official day as a teacher.

That first day of school with the students was probably the longest day of my life. There were so many students and names that everything seemed like a blur. It seemed as if every child had an exception to where they could (or could not) sit, what they were willing to do, and what they were going to allow me to do. The more parents kept interrupting my instruction to bring their children to school, the more frazzled I became. Every class period I was charged with not only engaging the students who wanted to be there, but I also had to reach the students who couldn't care less about class. To make matters worse, every period I was sent a note from the office asking me for information I was clueless about. It was my first day of class!

    That first day as an educator made me realize the small things I took for granted as a student, such as the amount of stress my teachers were under while trying to ensure I received a quality education. Not to mention as a teacher I was responsible for everything my students did. Who knew just to go the restroom in high school students needed not only a pass, but also had to sign out of the class? If a student dared not come back in 10 minutes, I was scared they were skipping class and committing some type of atrocities in the building!

    Needless to say, by the end of the day I was a nervous wreck. I kept thinking I would be fired for letting kids go to the bathroom too often and I didn't even want to think about the student who left my room right before the bell without permission. I wondered if my principal could hear all the commotion coming from my room from me constantly rearranging my students' seating arrangement—who knows? But at 2:15, I literally sat in my chair, put my head in my hands and wondered if I had made the right decision. When I got home, my family dared not to ask my how my day went. As I lay down to go to sleep all I could think was, "The first day of school was hell."

The next morning I decided to come back to school for my second day in the classroom and from that point on I was totally consumed by teaching. There were days everything went wonderful, but there were days I wanted to lock myself into a room and cry. In the midst of my "on-the-job training," I was dealing with students who flat-out refused to listen, parents who questioned my qualifications because I looked too young, and the stresses of getting acclimated to a city I was still fairly new in.

Thankfully, I had two mentors who were veteran teachers, but they could not help me with everything—they had their own classrooms to prepare for. In an attempt to get a handle on things I tried to read the popular teaching books to get ideas on how to manage my classroom. But many of their ideas did not seem doable with kids who are old enough to know better than to be scared by that "teacher eye."

Here I was working in the inner city, where many of my kids came from homes where they would be the first person in their family to graduate from college. How in the world could I reach them by employing strategies that were so out of date?

Little did I know that my breaking point was coming.

> *"I don't like you, your class or this assignment."*
>
> *With those words, one of the most unruly students in my classes, Tanya*, decided to slam her book closed and look at me to see what my next move would be. As I looked at her, I could do one of two things: address her rudeness or ignore her and continue to facilitate the reading of the classic, The Crucible.*
>
> *As much as I dreaded even having a conversation with her, I had to respond for the sake of not losing the rest of my class.*
>
> *I paused then carefully leveled out my words. "I appreciate your feedback, Ms. Jones, but right now we'd really love for you to read your part of Tituba."*
>
> *The student glared at me and I knew she wanted to make a bigger scene but right at that moment another vocal student yelled, "Girl, if you don't read, we're about to all have a problem with you!"*
>
> *Tanya gave me the nastiest look she could, opened her book, and reluctantly began to read her part.*
>
> *I had won this battle but there would be plenty of days like this—with this student and others.*

*Names of students have been changed throughout the book.

2
My Breaking Point

Educating teenagers is hard because often they come to school believing they already know everything about everything. As a new teacher, I did not know what to expect. But after the "newness" wore off, I found that there were a couple of students who seemed to have only one goal in life—to make my life hard. In particular, there was an unruly student named Tatyana who took me to my point of no return.

From day one, she decided that she was going to give me a hard time. She was constantly disruptive. She would curse, talk out of turn, and attempt to upset the other students with her shenanigans. I would call her mother (following advice from other teachers), but that did not help because her mother was equally rude. Every time I called home, the mother would blame me for Tatyana's behavior. One afternoon her mother even came to the school and threatened to get me fired. I was called to the office halfway through my planning period to see Tatyana's mother sitting in my principal's office glaring at me with her daughter's most recent progress report in her hand. As my principal tried to facilitate a reflective discussion on Tatyana's behavior, her mother was not having it and constantly interrupted us as we presented evidence of Tatyana's bad behavior.

    Instead of acknowledging her daughter's disruptive behavior, she attempted to put the blame on me. She even reasoned that my dislike of Tatyana resulted in her receiving a C opposed to an A. She refused to admit that not only was Tatyana behind in her reading, but she was having difficulties in all of her classes. Sitting there unable to get a word in my defense, I was tired of my professionalism being questioned. As soon as the "conference" was over, I packed up my bag and walked out the building with little more than a "bye" to anyone. I was sick and tired of being blamed for attempting to make kids behave.

    As I drove home from work that day, I considered just handing over my keys the next day and choosing another profession where mental abuse was not the norm. In what other job can people make baseless attacks on your character without any type of personal responsibility? Apparently, this happens in education. While I was mad about my experience with this parent and student, I had colleagues at other schools that told me horror stories of parents attacking teachers and threatening them when things did not go their way. I was officially disgusted.

    As I drove to my apartment, I had an epiphany as I stopped by my local ice cream shop to drown my sorrows in chocolate. I thought, *These are kids. Why am I allowing them to get me upset? For now on, it's either me or the students.* The more I thought about the previous conference, I realized that I was not in the wrong, but if I was going to survive I would have to try something different. I refused to work in an environment where I was not respected. So either the kids were going to get in line or I was going to quit my job. The choice was mine.

For the rest of the night I sat up and analyzed why I was having so much trouble with certain children in my classroom. After reflecting on my own experiences in school, I realized I respected the teachers who demanded that respect. The reality was that I was not demanding my respect.

Fast forward to the issues I was having in my classroom. Students were not being held accountable for their actions. The solution was seemingly simple. I had to show them who was boss and that started with establishing structure.

To say it lightly, the lack of structure in my class was causing problems. To make matters worse, I was working with teens who sometimes could not see the value in homework, projects, or good behavior. The answers were not in books from my graduate school classes—the answers were in my classroom. I was going to figure this out myself. That next morning, after meeting with my principal, I was ready for war.

Operation "Get Those Children in Line" had begun.

Instead of starting class with some fun warm-up, I decided to get some order. I stood outside my door and made all of the students line up before they were allowed to come in the classroom. Any rowdy student who attempted to enter my room was redirected back into the hallway they came from and told they could come into my room once they had learned to conduct themselves properly. I then stood there while at least five (the usual misfits) complained as usual. Unfazed, I reminded them that they would receive a zero in my class and be subjected to a hall sweep if they were still in the hallway when the bell rang. While kids were being redirected in the hallway, the other kids were busy trying to find their new seats. Yes, they now had a seating chart that was displayed on my projector. As soon as the bell rang, I shut the door and began teaching.

Students were shocked. I kept hearing, "Mrs. Warren, what are we doing?" I continued teaching. Five minutes later, I heard a student say, "Guys, she not playing with us anymore. I'm about to do my work!"

One by one, students decided they better get started with notes before they were too far behind. If students attempted to make a ruckus or distract the class, I would point to the door and make a "zero" motion so they would know their consequences. Kids who were in the hallway started to come in, and they had no choice but to sit quietly and do their work because that was what everyone else was doing.

I guess word had spread fast that I was going crazy. I noticed my assistant principal kept peeping into my classroom. She must have noticed I was not in a good mood because she disregarded the students in the hallway, and I continued to regain control of my classroom. By the end of the period, almost 99% of the students were busily working. For every class period, I did the same thing. All my students (including Tatyana) were on task and listening.

The next day I did the same thing, except when they came in the classroom, I handed them a revised syllabus with my new policies and procedures, and immediately I went over what was expected in my class. Then we went to work again. Slowly, word began to spread that I actually knew what I was doing and kids began to realize certain things were not going to fly in my classroom. During the first month of my "lock down," I had plenty of conferences with my kids, parents, and even my principal, but I wasn't budging. In the process of reining in the disorder in my class, I was building relationships with students and parents. Before long, students were correcting themselves. I had finally taken control of my class.

My crisis had been averted.

To other new teachers, I had performed a miracle in getting unruly students to pay attention and be alert in class. I just did what every effective teacher does from day one:

- I developed relationships with my students. Whether good or bad, students knew that I cared and this made them want to "act right" the majority of the time.
- I maximized my instructional time in my class. Students no longer had time to act up.
- I set high expectations for my students and dared one of them to break them.
- I decided I was the boss, not my students.

On the other side of town

Things were not going as well for my friends at other schools in the same district. They were struggling. Many had quit, while others had decided to "cower in the corner" and pray for the school year to end quickly. Some were scared of their students and so discouraged by their administrator's lack of discipline they either walked out on the job or got fired by the end of the year.

I can specifically remember a close friend of mine calling me one afternoon in early October completely discouraged and disgusted with teaching. She told me a story of her principal calling her name over the school intercom to chastise her because she allowed some students to the bathroom without a hall pass. To top things off, she was frustrated because her students refused to do any work in her biology class. They frequently skipped her class and when they did show up, they were so disruptive that often she just sat in the back of the classroom and only helped kids who wanted to learn. Within the first three months of school, she had to call the school resource officer to her room to remove a parent during a conference due to being threatened. Things were getting rough.

I tried to comfort her and give her tips, but her desire to teach was gone. She left the district during Christmas break. I asked her later what could have helped her stay in the classroom. "I needed support and no one really wanted to give that to me," she said.

This got me thinking. Why aren't teachers supported when they are having issues in a classroom? Why is it assumed something is wrong with the teacher if students are unruly and defiant? Why are parents not held accountable for what their children do while at school? Could a child go into a store and curse out the manager, refuse to pay for their items, and still be invited back to shop there? Of course not. So why do we allow it in public education? Why do we allow so many good teachers to leave just because they may need help?

This thought nagged at me after I left my first teaching job and went into a larger urban district and saw the same thing happening. What could be done to help retain effective teachers? I saw administrators giving teachers how-to books that employed elementary strategies for teachers who taught middle and high school students. Needless to say, the majority of self-help books for teachers would be better used as door stoppers than to help teachers in the battlefield—the classroom.

After nearly thinking about this for over a decade, I decided it was time to tell my story. I gained my expertise through going to work over 18,000 days over the last 10 years. I gained my expertise by working in schools with populations of students that are the most underserved in this country. I learned to be an expert.

There was a knock on my door. As I got up to answer it, there was an older man with a police badge at my door with a student who looked like my class was the last place he wanted to be.

"Mrs. Warren, here is your new student," the man said, skipping introductions. "If he misses your class or is more than ten minutes late, please call and email me immediately." He handed me his card and left. As I looked at my new student, I asked his name.

"Johnny." His answer was short without any emotion.

In my best teacher voice, I said, "Okay, Johnny take a seat and I'll set you up with what the class is doing." Luckily, my students were finishing the movie, "The Odyssey" so Johnny seemed to be interested in the content.

When the class was over, I managed to hand Johnny a study guide before he left my class. As I was collecting the rest of my papers, one of my students lingered behind.

"What's wrong, Chevon?" I asked as I busily prepared for my next class.

"Mrs. Warren, you should be careful with Johnny," she said quietly.

I looked up surprised. "Why?"

"Because he lives in my neighborhood and he just got out of juvenile for carjacking someone."

I could have dropped my computer right there, but I held my composure.

"Thanks, Chevon. I'll remember that."

She quickly left the room and I sat in my chair. What in the hell had I gotten myself in to?

3

So You Got The Job—Now What?

There is a myth that college prepares potential teachers to be in the classroom. The public believes that somewhere in college classrooms across America, teachers are taught how to prepare for students. Some may even believe teachers go through drills to know what to expect in the classroom, but this is the farthest thing from the truth. I graduated college in December and by August, I was walking into the classroom getting ready to teach a classroom full of children. I knew content, but I was seriously lacking in pedagogy.

After my hellacious first day of school (and due to No Child Left Behind mandates that I needed to be Highly Qualified) I enrolled in a master's program in Instruction and Curriculum. However, I never really learned how to deal with what was happening in my classroom. Professors shied away from telling me how to manage the student who was on probation and who couldn't care less if they received a zero on an assignment. They were flabbergasted when I described how some of my parents had literally checked out from their child's education. During most of my classes, I thought about how out of touch colleges were to what was actually happening in the classroom.

I only learned how to handle difficult situations by being in the classroom, watching, and talking to other teachers. When Johnny* came to my class, I was not a new teacher. I had taught for five years so despite the other student's warning, I figured that I would treat him with respect and we would both get along. In class, he was quiet and mainly sat and observed what me and the other students did. While he was not disruptive in my class, he gave the other (new) teacher hell. Equally, the new teacher was very paranoid due to his prior arrest records. Her short teacher training had not helped her prepare for students like Johnny.

One of the problems with teacher training is that many professors cannot address the nuts and bolts of what to expect in schools because they have not been in a classroom in decades. Even worse, some professors have never been in a public school classroom other than to observe.

If you are fortunate to be hired before the school year starts, you may have time to get ready but the reality is that many teachers are hired mid-year. So what do you do when you have signed your contract and you may not even know your assigned school? Do you spend your summer relaxing for the upcoming year or do you actively start to build on your foundation of being a teacher?

I recommend getting in the trenches and begin your foundation as a teacher. When school starts, there is no time to do the majority of housekeeping things you need to do before the school year starts, especially for new teachers. Before I was able to get in my classroom, I took time to familiarize myself with my school so that when I received students similar to Johnny* I was somewhat prepared.

I was able to ask questions, look at the curriculum, and really determine what I wanted my classroom to look like. Before the kids come back to school, I recommend the following activities to get ready for the year:

- Read the state standards for your content area. They should be second knowledge to you.
- Brainstorm activities you would like to do with the kids. Use resources like Pinterest and education blogs to peek into classrooms across the country.
- Familiarize yourself with the district you will be teaching in. Read the district's website, the local newspaper, and other resources to give you a clear vision of the district's goals and mission.
- If you are already aware of the classes you will teach, go online to look at sample assignments from teachers across the country.

- Read any necessary materials that kids will be responsible for reading during the school year.
- Meet your co-workers so you can know everyone before the school year.
- Research any high-stakes testing you will be responsible for in your content area.
- Meet with your principal or assistant principal so you can understand expectations, duties, etc.
- Talk with veteran teachers to get their advice after being in the classroom.

These are all suggestions to help you come into the school year with some knowledge of what is expected from you since you will be expected to know these things on the first day of classes. Too often teachers are thrown into the lion's den during the first week of school and they end up behind on work before they even start! Be smart. Use your time wisely. The summer before I started teaching I was introduced to the other teachers in my department over informal meetings orchestrated by my building principal. During our meetings I was able to find out crucial information about my school that I would need later. That teaching was going to be overwhelming.

Once the summer is over, the time that most students dread is here—the start of school. Before big budget cuts, teacher in-service lasted a week, but now in-service may only be three days long. For new teachers especially, in-service is a time where teachers, principals, and school staff get the school ready to open for the kids. During that week, there are meetings about everything from curriculum to procedures for the school. Often this is the first time teachers find out what they are teaching and what their classrooms look like.

In between all the meetings there should be time for you to get things ready for the students. With so much time on our hands, it is easy to lose track of time and have to spend the weekend before school opens in your classroom. In the next chapters, you will find out what to do *before* the students report to your classroom. Read, take notes, and have a great school year!

"And don't go here or there, or you will be sorry." My roommate, Kristy, was driving as she pointed to all the areas in the city of Memphis that I needed to stay away from. As a new transplant to the city, I was happy she took time to let me know the areas that were deemed unsafe, but I kept thinking to myself, *"Then what areas are safe?"*

As we drove through the city, I remember seeing what's normal for many inner-city areas: abandoned buildings, housing projects, liquor stores, and people on the streets. I wasn't scared, but I was curious about the rich history of downtown Memphis right around the National Civil Rights Museum.

Four years later, I would learn that area very well as I began to teach students from that community. Instead of riding by and wondering about people's lives, I would drive through the area and worry about my students who lived this reality.

4

The Community Is Your School

One of the best things I did after working in a "high needs" area was to disconnect the images I saw on the news and take the time to find out what my school community was really like. I quickly learned that the school in which you teach is a microcosm of the community in which it is located. Often we forget how influential a community can be on the school. Sometimes the school mimicking the community is a good thing; other times it throws a wrench in what the school is trying to do for the community members.

If there are problems in the community, those same problems show up in the school. At one school I taught in, the community was ravaged by gang violence. In school, we had to fight the same issue before we could do any teaching. We would frequently see students engage in fights from students in rival gangs. So to help ease tension and start a dialogue, I taught classics like *The Outsiders* for students to understand that their community issues were not unique and that neighborhood rivalries were as old as their parents. As a school community we had to adopt a zero-tolerance policy for anything gang related. I would say that at least 20 percent of our school day revolved on keeping certain students separated and having mediations between groups just to be able to teach.

It is crucial for new teachers to understand the communities they are teaching in and to be proactive about issues that may arise. As a new teacher, I had no clue about the area that I was teaching in and I suffered because of it. Teaching in a historical city like Memphis, it was imperative for me to know a bit of the history of the city. Despite housing the beautiful National Civil Rights Museum in honor of Dr. Martin Luther King, Jr., this was still a segregated city and the schools were proof. There were serious inequities between schools on opposite sides of town. The school I started in was a small school developed by the district to give kids who had "difficulties" in their home schools a place to finish their education.

Even though the school was downtown, kids from all over the city attended. Some kids were clearly middle class, while some were homeless. Everyone had a story. Some kids came after being expelled from their last school, while others wanted the chance to attend a different school. Within my first six months in the classroom, I got to see firsthand how a student's home environment dictated everything they did once they left the house.

One particular student, Tina, stayed after school with me every day for tutoring. Whenever it came time to leave, she was always hesitant to walk home, despite living a quick five-minute drive from the school. After listening to her excuses, I agreed to take her home to see if I could find out the problem.

Upon getting in the car and driving two minutes, I immediately knew why she was scared to walk home by herself.

There were countless abandoned warehouses and random people roaming the street on the way home. In addition, due to Daylight Savings Time, it was getting dark earlier and there were plenty of places for seedy people to hide. I could tell she was relieved to have a ride home and not have to be scared. When I dropped her off at her apartment, her mother came out to thank me for taking time to bring her baby home. From then on, I told that particular student to come to Saturday school so I could make sure she could get home safely without worrying about walking home in the dark. Without driving through that neighborhood that evening, I would have never learned the reason behind her fear. Knowing the community we teach in is crucial to reaching the students.

As a new teacher, it was important for me to know what exactly was in the neighborhood the kids were coming from. It helped as I assigned projects or tried to decide what community service projects I would have students complete at the end of the year. As a teacher, it is important to know not just the students' names but:

- the makeup of the community they are from
- the dynamics of the school and community around it
- the feeder school the kids are coming from.

Once I educated myself about the community of every school I taught in, the fewer problems I had in the classroom. Every year as the school year starts, I see new teachers who have absolutely no clue about the kids they are teaching. How can you teach content to a child whom you know nothing about? Would you buy a new beauty product and have no idea how to use it or where it came from? Would you send a loved one to a medical facility without researching the doctors? Of course not. In the education field, there is no difference. In order to be an effective teacher you must get to know your students—this will give you a unique perspective on why kids come to school with so many issues.

Another crucial aspect of being in the classroom is learning about the families our children come from. In my first school, parental involvement was average, but as I worked in other schools, I learned that parental involvement is a luxury, especially in high school. There have been times where despite my constant calling, parents will not call me back to deal with classroom behaviors and I am forced to have the school social worker attempt to make contact with the parent.

Once I have finally met the parents, it's usually very clear on why the student behaves a certain way. I will never forget sitting in an IEP meeting with a student and listening to the parent speak so negatively about the child in front of them. So disheartened by the parent's negativity, we had to ask the student to step outside the rom and have a talk with the parent about positive parenting. It was no wonder that this child was struggling in school.

Later in my career, I had a child who was a constant disruption in class. He was consistently off task, disruptive to other students, and failing his classes. As a grade level team we met with him numerous times and called his parents but to no avail. The child continued to act out. At the end of the year he failed the majority of his classes so before he could register, the school insisted his parents visit the school. His father came and instantly the boy who was so disruptive in class was shy and embarrassed. Dad slurred his words, talked extra loud, and basically told us that his son was responsible for his handicapped brother after school and that he had no time for homework or fun at all. Leaving the conference made me understand the young man's struggle. It also made me realize that this child needed positive support and time to be a child.

Another way to understand the community where you teach is to understand the "feeder schools" the students come from. Feeder schools are the previous level schools that the majority of your students will come from. Usually you will have one or two elementary schools and one middle school that all students feed into a high school. Understanding the culture at the feeder schools allows you to be prepared for the students you are going to get in your classroom. As a school community, once we began to look at trends at those schools, we were better equipped to teach students in high school.

As a new teacher, take time to get to know your students and community using these basic strategies: get out in the community, call and introduce yourself to a parent, arrange early parent-teacher conferences, and listen when the children speak about the community!

Get out in the community

After teaching for a number of years, I decided to relocate to a bigger city to an even larger district. I knew that the school I would be working at was considered a "Title 1" school, but I thought it was important for me see the school myself. While teaching at a new school is a daunting task, teaching in a new city can seem like an impossible task. To try to calm my nerves, I tried to do several things to "get to know" my new students and the neighborhood where the school was located. The first thing I did was to drive around the immediate neighborhood at various times of the day and take mental notes of the things I observed. Unlike other communities, I noticed that not only were there limited eateries but popular stores like Wal-Mart and Target were 20-25 minutes away. While economic establishments were scarce, there were community centers, churches and several liquor and "corner" stores. The epicenter of the community was a lone Kmart that looked like it had seen better days. It was obviously an underserved community.

Simply put, this meant that my kids were coming from an area where there were limited resources. That did not mean that I expected less from my students, but it did mean that I understood it may be harder for them to jump on the bus and go to a Target or Wal-Mart to get needed supplies for projects. It also helped me understand the perspectives my students may have coming into my class.

Another good strategy to use to learn about the community is to research the crime in the area using the local police department's website. In every school I have worked in, I have completed my research and am always astounded by the results. I have always worked in an area that may have a high amount of crime so when I looked at results from this particular area, I knew from the majority of crime (robbery, murder, prostitution, etc) that these children would likely come to school with a lot of issues and that school may be the last thing on their mind. Knowing all of this allowed me to acclimate to the school much faster than other teachers who started with me.

After finding a lot of disheartening data, it may be easy for some to rationalize that some children were "unreachable" and that learning would not take place. However, for me, it reinforced that I had to teach like my life depended on it and that I had to be firm yet fair.

Introduce yourself to parents

As the first day of school started, I was excited to finally meet the students that I took so much time to learn about. I quickly saw that even though this was a new school, many of the issues I encountered at earlier schools would be the same. Despite these issues in the community, I did notice that our teachers and staff tried to lessen the impact those social issues had on our students. In addition, we also had a strong set of parents who tried to support our students in any way possible.

During the first month of school, I usually make it a point to call all of my parents and introduce myself and my class. Since I have a lot of students, I break my calls up into about five to ten a day and I simply let them know how they can get a hold of me and if there is anything I need to know about their child. While these calls are time consuming, I find out great information about my students from their parents. Parents have let me know all kinds of things—that their child suffers from a mental disorder or letting me know of cases of bullying in younger grades!

Listen to your students

While data has a purpose, one of the most important aspects of teaching is to actually learn about your students. Contrary to beliefs, high school students are very eager to tell you who they are. At times, you can ask those questions about where they come from, but it's helpful to use creative strategies to learn about their lives and what they value:

- I gave my students interest surveys.
- I allowed students to write about their families and communities as a writing diagnostic.
- I listened to them. It's amazing what you can learn from your students when you listen to the quiet conversations that occur while students are working independently.

This human data actually allowed me to learn about my students' needs and how to teach accordingly. I strongly believe that the majority of kids want to learn and most importantly, many of them displayed extreme resilience in spite of crushing issues they wrote about. I looked at all of my students—some were on probation, others who were the breadwinners in their homes, and the others who badly wanted to go to college. In the end, it was my responsibility to learn about my students—before school and after they come. It will help you understand student's behaviors and help your job as a classroom teacher.

"Before I can hire you, I want you to interview with two of our ELA teachers."

This is what my principal told me when I interviewed with her. I had no clue what that interview was going to be like, but I found myself driving to meet these teachers in the middle of June.

Surprisingly the interview with the other teachers was laid-back. Both women were a lot younger than I thought they were. I had imagined them to be little old ladies with a no-nonsense attitude. I figured they liked to scare new teachers with horror stories. But for the next couple of hours, my interview felt like a really good lunch conversation. We laughed, I asked questions, they asked questions, and I was hired.

Little did I know that in less than 60 days, I would need these ladies like my life depended on it.

5

Veteran Teachers Are Not The Enemy

One of the most popular misconceptions of education reform advocates is that veteran teachers hold no value. This is the farthest from the truth in every school that I have ever taught. The veteran teachers helped me develop a toolkit for my teaching and become a leader in my profession. However, I can admit that sometimes it can be intimidating to know that your co-worker has taught longer than you have been alive! At the first school I ever taught at, I was the only new teacher in the building. This made my journey even more difficult, because I thought everyone from my principal to my co-workers would have me under a microscope. My principal, being the mind reader and observer she was, quickly connected me to two veteran teachers who helped me survive those first two years in the building. For them I will always be grateful.

There were several teachers in the building who been in the classroom for more than 20 years, while others had worked in the school district in several different capacities for several decades. If the stress of having to learn about students is not enough, it does not compare with coming into a building and becoming colleagues with teachers who have been educating children for longer than I had been alive! I expected to be the outcast in the school, but I was lucky enough to be welcomed with open arms. It was always nice to see someone run a classroom like a well-oiled machine while you are struggling to take roll!

By observing veteran teachers, not only can you learn invaluable lessons, but you can survive your first year teaching and learn some new "tricks" to get you through days like my first day of school. During my first two years in the classroom, my two mentors taught me all of the unwritten rules of the school that I would have never learned in a college classroom or in a handbook. These rules helped me survive that year at school without offending everyone in the building. Here are a few of the lessons I was taught:

- I needed to have tutorial at least once a week to avoid the principal thinking I was a slacker.
- There were parking spots reserved for the older teachers who didn't like to walk far to get into the building.

- If I complimented the lunch staff, they would give me the better cut of the meat.
- Be firm, yet fair.
- I needed to get the office staff small gifts on Appreciation Days.
- Avoid writing a lot of frivolous discipline write-ups and the assistant principal would likely take my concerns seriously.

While these things may seem trivial, you need to learn these "unspeakable" rules as a new teacher so that you can get along with people on staff. These veteran teachers also helped me interact with students who were known to be difficult to new teachers. I liked to go into the veteran teacher's classroom and observe the student who refused to do work in my room, but excelled in their classroom. Watching these veteran teachers allowed me reevaluate policies and structures that I had in my classroom.

Both of my mentors had (combined) about 20 years in the classroom and their approaches were different, yet effective. One was very diplomatic and always maintained a very calm demeanor even in times when students drove her crazy. She had been educated at some of the top schools and I admired how she was willing to do the work and not rely on her top-notch training. My other mentor was the exact opposite. She was animated in the classroom and the kids loved it. She had a long history in the district and I appreciated sitting with her and learning about all the politics in the district. By talking with both of them, I was able to learn strategies that still help me in the classroom today.

For example, I had a student from hell, Sally, who questioned my authority constantly from the first day of class. In addition, this student was loud, obnoxious, and constantly wanted to be the center of attention in the classroom. Fed up by her behavior and tired of assigning her detention, one of my mentors told me all I had to do was get in touch with her father. By chance the next day she got into an argument with a girl in class so I decided to call her father—right there as the students worked independently .As I dialed his number Sally was increasingly getting quieter and quieter. Luckily, I got a hold of him on the first try. While he was not very chatty, he ended the call with a terse, "She will no longer be a problem." The next day, Sally came into class giving me nasty looks, but she was no longer a disruption. She was mad at me for a while, and one day she came to my desk and said, "You got me in trouble, Ms. Warren." But I never had another problem with her.

Teaching is not meant to be a one-person sport—it is designed to be a team sport. Once you have a good team, the whole school works better. I made it a point to go and talk to my mentor teachers on a daily basis. However, I got lucky. Not every mentor/mentee relationship is this fulfilling.

One of the most important lessons I learned from my mentors was how to deal with parents, especially ones who may not be as kind when first meeting a new teacher. Both teachers had a way with words to diffuse even the most tense situations (like when a parent comes yelling in the office because her "baby" received an F). They could also make the parents feel like they had an ally with them. While my experience with my mentors was great, other staff members were not as friendly.

On any staff, there are always a few teachers who do not warm up to "new blood" right away. Sometimes there are things like not saying hello in the morning or purposely saying insensitive things. While I was offended, I realized that really I needed to prove that I could work in that environment and not run out of the room crying because a child upset me. While I was "earning my respect," I also used the following tips to connect me to other veteran teachers:

1. **I asked for their advice.** Teachers love to talk so I would ask questions on everything from how to set up my grade book to how to deal with a pain-in-the-neck parent. Some of the answers may have been questionable, but for the most part, I got really good, honest advice.
2. **I sat in the teacher's lounge at least once a week, listening to their struggles.** The common misconception is that the teacher's lounge is a "black hole" of sorts and all teachers do

there is gossip and complain. In my experiences, I liked the teacher lounge because there I learned that despite being the new teacher on staff, there were others who were struggling with the kids. Often I would just sit back, listen, and take away helpful hints for my classroom.

3. **I joined the Teacher's Union to connect with experienced teachers across the district.** In the first district I taught in, the union was very strong in helping teachers. So I joined and was immediately introduced to people who had been in the district for decades and could answer questions that I had. In addition, getting involved in the union exposed this young college graduate to the political side of teaching and really exposed me to the negotiations that took place just to make sure teachers had a suitable environment to teach.

Contrary to what a lot of teacher preparation programs might teach, I did not go in thinking I was already the expert teacher. Some may think because we learned the new and upcoming strategies that we are somewhat better than veteran teachers are. I took the opposite stance: If teachers have survived in a system for decades, they obviously are doing something right.

I encourage all new teachers to get to know the teachers they work with. The old cliché, "There is no I in team," seems corny but in reality that's one of the best mottos in education. With the profession being so hard, it is almost crucial for teachers to stick together in the building. During my 13 years in the classroom, I have made lifelong friends who have helped me in my times of need, celebrated birthdays with me, and even celebrated the birth of my children. I can never thank them enough for everything they have done for me.

"Your total is $550.00." The cashier finished ringing up my order as I sat shocked that I had just racked up that much in buying supplies for my classroom.

I had only bought cleaning supplies, manipulatives, posters, classroom supplies, a classroom carpet, a set of novels, and a couple of extra items. It couldn't possibly add up to over $350 dollars.

"Ma'am...How are you going to pay for this?"

I looked at the pile and answered, "Umm, yes, I can pay using two types of payments." When I got home I was sick that I had used my hard earned money to buy school supplies, but I reasoned surely the school would reimburse me once I showed them receipts.

When I got to my school the next day, I quickly got my feelings hurt after asking the school secretary how I could get my money back.

"No, Ms. Lane, we don't reimburse teachers for their supplies due to budget constraints. You may want to see what the previous teacher left in the room and work with that.'

As I walked back to my room, I knew that from that point on, I'd have to be a lot more cautious in what I bought for my classroom and where I shopped. Upon looking, I found some things I could do.

By 6:00 p.m., I had already returned my previous day's supplies and had searched the dollar store and our local thrift store to furnish my classroom.

Never again would I go "broke" trying to decorate my room.

6

Don't Break The Budget!

One of the great things about being a teacher is that often you get a space that is just yours—a classroom that you can decorate how you want. Most teachers make their classroom an extension of their homes since they spend at least 180 days a year there. However, no one enjoys furnishing their classroom when it can seriously put them in debt.

My first few years of being in the classroom, I would spend hundreds of dollars to make sure that my classroom was perfect. I rarely found any deals, and by year three I was tired of always using my money to furnish my space. I knew that I would have to do something to relieve my pockets.

It is common practice for teachers spend their own setting up their classrooms for their students. Sometimes they are reimbursed for their expenses, but in most districts, the teachers are on their own. So how can you decorate your classroom without going broke? Start by researching organizations that help teachers. Around the start of every school year, newspapers, websites, and television commercials are inundated with advertisements for cheap crayons, reams of paper, and pencils. As teachers, we go mad for $.01 pencils, while the average citizen will disregard these advertisements. Teachers understand just how valuable watching ads can be for our classrooms.

All teachers need basic supplies like paper, bulletin board supplies, etc. But, what about first-aid kits, air freshener, and Lysol wipes that teachers will need? Those are the items no one thinks about as they're furnishing their rooms. Trust me—all it takes is for a child to get a bad paper cut or get bitten by a bug in class and you will see how important it is to have a first-aid kit in your classroom.

So what is the key? It's important to begin to stock up on supplies even before the kids come. Use these steps to spend wisely without going broke:

Find programs that will sponsor teacher supplies

Start by doing a simple Internet search about programs to help supply teachers with supplies. Then simply sign up online and the program will send you certain supplies. In Georgia, we use Kids in Need (www.kinf.org), but there are other national programs as well. One note: sometimes you'll receive supplies you cannot use for your grade level/content area, but use those items to barter with other teachers for items they do not need.

Ask your students to contribute to the fund

This seems to be an easier task for elementary school teachers, but after noticing how many supplies I bought for my son, I decided to start a wish list for supplies in my class. Even though I taught in high school, I sent out my list at the start of every semester and I let the parents know them contributing was completely voluntary. Not every student brought the supplies, but it was enough to help me survive until the next semester.

Buy supplies in bulk from wholesale suppliers

Shopping at warehouse stores are a good way for teachers to buy supplies in bulk—it often costs less than if you go to the regular store. I usually stock up on items like Kleenex, Lysol Spray, air fresheners—just so I can start off with a good supply.

Use coupons to get needed supplies

While clipping coupons can be time consuming, it is worth it if you can get a bag full of supplies for pennies on the dollar. While I am not a big coupon clipper, I know teachers who collect coupons all summer just to supply their classrooms with much needed supplies.

Shop thrift stores and yard sales for supplies

One time I needed a small couch for my class's reading nook. Instead of spending hundreds of dollars on one, I went to a couple of yard sales and found one for $30 bucks. Once I cleaned it and let it air out, I had a beautiful place for my students to read.

In the end, all teachers need supplies and often there is no school budget to get what you need. It is important to be creative in how you get your supplies during the year. Do not be shy about asking other teachers if they know any affordable ways to get free supplies.

So what happens when you have your supplies? Do you just stockpile them at your house or stuff them in your cabinet at school? Of course, you should put them to use and one of the easiest things to do is to follow these steps.

If at all possible, have your classroom ready before the start of in-service training. When I first started teaching, my main goal was to have my room available about two weeks before school started. Luckily, I had an understanding principal who would give me access to my room so I could start to start to set up for the year.

Once I had access to my room, I managed my time so I was only in the room for two or three hours at maximum until my work was complete. That was enough time for me get what I needed done but most importantly, it still allowed time to get my mind together so that I wasn't mad about coming to school when I was supposed to be on vacation.

The first day back in the classroom, I always took inventory on what I already had and what I need to get my room together. This usually resulted in me spending a full day running around town trying to get supplies for cheap. Once I had all needed materials, I begin setting up my classroom. Even though I teach high school, I try to have an inviting space for my students so that takes work. I bring in a big piece of carpet. I have a reading corner. I display past student's works, and I add pictures of my family on my desk for the kids to see.

Every piece of furniture that I buy for my classroom is secondhand. What I had to understand when setting up my classroom was to get smart if I needed something. For smaller items, I utilize my colleagues. At first, I would go out into the store and buy what I needed, but that got expensive. Now before I buy anything, I walk around my floor and ask if other teachers have it. Then usually we trade for something they need. This allows me to help another teacher while also helping myself. I also realized that there is a point when you can go overboard in decorating your room. It can distract students from paying attention because there is so much going on in the classroom.

To keep things to a minimum, I always have the following sections in my room:

- a reading corner
- student work corner
- computer stations
- conference station
- "paper" station (for students to pick up if they were absent/ late, turn in work, etc.).

Being organized allows me start the year on a good foot and shows the kids that I care about the space I will be in for the next 180 days. I noticed if a teacher's room is messy, kids automatically assume that a teacher is disorganized.

During those first days of school, I spend time to make sure kids are acquainted with my classroom's set up. Sometimes this takes a while. In the end, I always take a lot of time to make sure my room is clean, organized, and ready to go.

"You live here?" I said it before I could stop myself as I took one of my students home from tutorial. We had just driven through a dilapidated area near downtown Memphis and all I saw were abandoned buildings and homeless people.

"No, right there!" My student laughed and pointed to a row of houses tucked away from the naked eye. "You thought you were going to have to get the school social worker, didn't you?" she said, jokingly as she got out the car. I laughed nervously, but I knew she was fortunate that she actually had somewhere to go home to.

In my first decade of teaching, I had seen students who were homeless and taking care of themselves. While I was glad that it was dark and I couldn't see everything, I remembered that despite me judging her situation, the kids' lives were real.

As I drove home to my side of town, I couldn't help but think about my student who lived in various hotels because his mother didn't have a steady job. He came to school and showered in the locker rooms and our coach washed his clothes for him daily. I also thought about my student who was brilliant but homeless after her mother put her out after finding out she was pregnant. As I got home, hugged my child, and made my family dinner, I always thought about my kids who I knew were struggling to find somewhere to stay for the night. Who would protect those kids?

For some kids, crime, poverty, and hopelessness wasn't something they just saw on television. It was right in their own homes.

7

Assumptions: How Many Of Us Have Them?

Working in a Title 1 public high school, it is easy to have assumptions about the students you teach and the people you work with. While I have always been lucky enough to work with teachers and students of all backgrounds, sometimes working in a high-poverty school breeds misconceptions. While social issues such as poverty, homelessness, and crime are in almost every school, the media assumes that low-income kids are difficult to manage or may not want to learn. Each school has its unique challenges and having preconceived assumptions can make those challenges multiply.

The kids I have worked with have been some of the smartest, kindest kids I have ever been around—once I "peeled" away their defenses. When I first started teaching, one of the first things I vowed was that I was going to hold my kids to the same standards my teachers held to me during school.

One of the first assumptions I made was that because my students were high needs that all of their home lives were bad. This was totally untrue. I taught several kids who were working and middle class students. Their parents worked every day just like me and they wanted their child to have a good education just like I wanted mine to have.

Just like you take time to learn who the students are, take time to get to know your co-workers with an unbiased mind. Many education programs today tell new teachers to not to get to know older teachers, but I say that they could be (and often are) your biggest help in the school. You may look at a teacher and assume (based on their appearance) that they cannot possibly know what they're talking about. Stop it. Get to know your co-workers and you will not regret it.

During my fifth year in the classroom, we had a new music teacher come to our school. He wasn't a new teacher, but he was new to the building. He was super jovial and was very entertaining, but it wasn't until I went to a show he had after school did I realize how talented he truly was. Here I was working with a man who was good enough to be paid for his music on the famous Beale Street. I was wrong to assume that he wasn't a true music professional. Later in my career, I happened to work with a teacher who liked to go against the norm and did the opposite of what the administration wanted her to do. She dressed everyday in jeans and her calm nature reminded me of the hippies that I saw in the movies. She was all about peace and love. One day I happened to go past her classroom and there she was totally engaging struggling Algebra 1 students with concepts that would blow your mind. Every student was engaged and she was doing the work of five teachers to help meet the needs of every student. No one would have ever known by looking at her that we had a math genius on our staff.

From all of these different co-workers, I learned that behind the teaching certificates are real people, with real talent and concerns. In the different schools and capacities I have worked in, I have always had good years when I have made a point to get to know my co-workers. Sometimes we arrange monthly social events or have impromptu meetings during the day to support one another when we have been particularly stressed.

School visits

I have always thought of the schools where I teach as one big playground of learning experiences. When I have time, I visit with other teachers in the building, not only to be friendly, but to add to my teaching repertoire. I usually ask teachers beforehand and when I come in, I make it a point to sit quietly in the back of class. I do not interact with the students. I just observe. So many times teachers are in schools and they literally feel like they are on an island. They do not know what the person next to them is doing much less the teacher on another hallway! I have worked in large and small schools and my best years are when I actually leave my classroom and explore.

I make it a point to observe teachers who teach different areas and grade levels. I cannot tell you how many times I've walked into someone's class and watched them teach an amazing lesson that made me go back into my room and try to do better!

So what if you are the person who stays to themselves and never goes outside the classroom? How do you get the courage to start visiting other rooms?

- Ask your fellow teachers.
- Schedule visits to make sure that teachers don't feel like you are in their room all the time.
- Do not interrupt the classroom flow.
- Send a note about all the positive things you noticed in the classroom.
- Keep your visits to a set time limit so you still have time to get things done.

"You can't be the teacher! You look young enough to be in high school!" one of my parents exclaimed on the first night of parent-teacher conferences. A month ago I would have cringed, but I was used to getting a hard time about my young appearance.

Before I could say anything, her child (my student) said, "She may look young, Mom, but she stays giving us some work!"

This example reminded me about how observant both my parents and teachers were about my appearance. Because I was only five years older than my juniors (unbeknownst to them), they were very curious about my life. They wanted to know if I was married, if I had kids, and if I listened to the same music as they did. They seemed to know I was young, but no one could put their finger on just how young I actually was. So I had to be swift and sarcastic with my remarks.

I always assured them that I was qualified with this statement, "Well, I may look young, but I assure you that I'm of age. What other reason would I have to wear a three-piece suit just to come to school?"

The kids would break out in laughter and I heard another student yell. "Okay, we're going to give you a chance, but if we find out that you're really our age, your grades don't count!"

As I started the conference, I chuckled in my head with how observant kids actually are.

8

Professionalism 101

As a child, the image that I had of my teachers were women who covered their bodies from head to toe, wore those thick-soled teacher shoes glasses and walked around the classroom with their ruler ready to pop a child who was off task. The majority of my teachers were Caucasian and I rarely had male teachers. In 2013, most teachers look nothing like that image. If you walk into any school in the country, you will notice teachers of a range of colors and ethnicities dressed in full suits or in slacks or khakis. As a new teacher, it was hard for me to figure out my professional standing in a building with teachers who were all so different.

Would I be the teacher who was covered up from head to toe with my "teacher shoes? Or would I be more laid back like Kevin Costner in the

1980s classic, *Summer School*? Would it be okay to show my tattoos or would I wear long-sleeved shirts year round to hide my life after school?

As a new teacher, I had no idea how I would present myself to my students. Watching the television classic portrayal of teachers, we are usually covered up from head to toe with our hair tied tightly in buns. On the other hand, you can look at satirical examples like in *Bad Teacher* where you see exaggerated examples of teachers in revealing outfits misbehaving in the classroom. While the latter may solicit laughter in the movie theater, it will quickly get you walked out of the building, unemployed.

So where is the balance while being in the classroom? Being a teacher does not require you dress in a suit every day, but it is necessary to dress as professionally as your content area allows. For example, if you are a kindergartner teacher it is almost impossible to wear a suit and tie everyday due to the messy projects you will be doing with your students. If you are a physical education teacher, you have to dress the part. The point is that it is important to find a way to dress comfortably and professionally. One of the first things I learned about teaching is that your outward appearance matters. Quite simply if you look good, you feel good.

Dress the part

As a new teacher at the ripe age of 22, I had no clue about what it meant to really dress as a teacher. At first, I came dressed up in a suit, but after trying to break up student altercations in a two-piece suit (complete with stockings and heels), I decided that maybe I needed to relax my clothing just a tad bit. At one point (after my feet were hurting tremendously) I almost bought a pair of those thick-soled teacher shoes. Finally I decided to have a comfortable mix of how I dressed. There are some days where I come in completely dressed up, while other days I opted for khaki pants and a nice button down top. No matter what I decide to wear, I always make sure I look professional. I never wore things that were too tight, short, or questionable.

    I learned early in my career that my mood was affected by how I dressed. If I dress professionally, I feel like a professional. If I know I do not look my best, then my day suffers. To stay organized and make sure I am presentable, I do little things that give me more time so I do not have to think about what I am wearing. The first and probably most important thing I do is lay my clothes out at the beginning of the week. This gives me more time to do other things (like lesson plans, phoning parents, etc.) that I need to get done.

    After you have figured out how to dress the part, it is important to have the right attitude when coming into the classroom. A good place to start is to realize that teachers have one of the most important jobs on the planet.

Know that your job is important and be confident in your pedagogy

Every morning for the past decade, I have repeated this mantra every morning: "I am doing the second-most important job in the world—teaching." Not everyone who becomes a teacher can do it effectively. Often it is not because they lack the skills but because they lack the confidence. I cannot tell you how many times I have seen teachers who are brilliant but who walk into the classroom without the confidence that they are the expert in the room.

Repeatedly when I have spoken to those teachers, they complain about all the variables in the classroom: the kids talk too much, they do not listen, etc. But I always counter with the obvious. Teachers go to school for their undergraduate degree, master's degree, and even PhDs—how are they not the experts in the classroom? Each morning, walk into that classroom breathe a sigh of relief. You are home; this is your classroom.

Take time to reassess your professional plan

The days are gone where teachers can teach for 30 years and then retire comfortably. Instead, teachers are being laid off and positions are being eliminated. There are teachers who are even unsure if they will ever teach full time again. So I implore you to develop a professional development plan for yourself that will allow you to be even more engaged with your content area. Use the Internet to find professional development through conferences, webinars, state department grants, etc. Apply for grants to attend these conferences and even consider presenting. All of these opportunities help you become a better professional.

Think of yourself as a brand

This is a difficult concept because for years teachers have been taught to think about themselves last. But just like a doctor or lawyer, educators are brands so we have to treat ourselves accordingly. Think about what you want people to know the most about you as an educator. Then make sure all of your actions support that vision.

Being a teacher is by far one of the hardest jobs on earth. We rarely receive recognition, our qualifications are always questioned, and our pay is always reduced. However, one of the things that teachers need to remember is that they should view themselves as a separate entity. If you did not work for your district, how could you build your professional profile? This may be you presenting at conferences, writing books about your content area, starting programs in your community, joining a professional organization, etc. Doing these things will make you feel like a professional despite the fact you may go into a building where morale is low and kids can be obnoxious.

One of the drawbacks of being an educator is that our professionalism is constantly tested. We are working with a client base that (at times) can be anything but professional. We deal with parents who will curse us out, state departments that many times do not respect our positions and media stories that paint us as lazy non-performers. Needless to say that at the end of the day it is easy to feel anything but professional when you are a teacher.

Teaching is hard, but never sacrifice your professionalism because that will invalidate all of the years of hard work that you have completed. Despite my challenges, I focused on my job and everything else came second. Take time and figure out your professional profiles—it will pay off!

> "Now let's look at Ms. Warren's lesson plans. As you can see they are detailed in narrative format. Maybe if you're having issues, you can maybe refer back to her to help you."
>
> These were the comments my principal made to another teacher during a faculty meeting that actually made me cringe. Other teachers in the school rolled their eyes, but as she continued to talk, I sunk further and further in my chair. It was meant as a compliment, but for a new teacher to be praised on her lesson plans, it made my life hard.
>
> Being the obsessive-compulsive person I was, for the first three years of my teaching career I did two sets of lesson plans. One was gave a quick glance and one was in-depth with a narrative for each activity.
>
> It would take me at least twelve hours every weekend to complete them. I wish I had learned to work smarter, not harder on lesson plans.

9

Lesson Plans: Don't Reinvent The Wheel

Instructional planning is an essential part of being an effective teacher. As a new teacher, you may plan for hours, while more veteran teachers will plan for shorter amounts of time. Despite the need for effective planning, lesson plans have the ability to be the thorn in every educator's behind. While it would be helpful if there was one universal form for everyone (regardless of content area or grade level) to complete, in reality lesson plan formats differ greatly from school to school, from grade level to content area. So what are new teachers supposed to do in order to get these plans complete, accurately?

Before I tell you what I did, let me tell you what *not* to do. My first year in the classroom I made two sets of lesson plans. One was on your standard form and the second one was a narrative of sorts that walked me through what I wanted to do. While it was helpful to me, it was also very time-consuming. So much so that I would spend my whole weekend, writing plans. I was working harder and not smarter. After being exhausted after looking at plans all weekend, I decided to make some changes and eventually I began to plan like a sane person.

For the new teacher use these steps to find your footing in lesson planning:

- First, approach your principal over instruction and curriculum and see what form the school uses.
- Before you create anything that has already been done, I suggest going to the people who teach your same content area and grade, and see if you can use/view/adjust their plans. This gives you a starting point to recreate, tweak or completely redo the plans. In many schools, teachers in the same content area and grade level teach the same thing so conferencing with your co-workers can help you determine what you need to do.

If you want to develop your own plans, take time to examine (and reexamine) your state's standards and then start to work on what you want your students to learn and how you can get them there. There are thousands of quality lesson plans all over the Internet. Take time and explore them so you can get ideas on how you want to use the content.

If the school year has not started yet, you have plenty of time to get your first unit together for the kids. Depending on your grade level, it is important to start your classroom content immediately and without hesitation. I taught high school for the past decade so every year I handed out the syllabus as the kids walked into the door and we immediately got to working on some great piece of literature or writing. I know many of you are thinking about diagnostic testing, but in many high schools across America, schedules are not correct until after the first week. So that whole first week we worked, and the second week we did diagnostic testing. In elementary and middle school, the schedule changes may not be so drastic so there may be more room to start the class off with testing.

While there are schools where unit planning is necessary, there are other schools where unit planning is not as crucial. Regardless of how your school views it, I recommend devoting a significant amount of time planning what you are planning to teach assess the content. It is important that material is paced accordingly and that you are prepared.

Even in my 13 years in the classroom, I still lesson plan but now I have a system. I write unit plans and then I use a calendar to document what I am going to do on a daily basis in the classroom. Since I have been in the classroom so long, I tweak assessments and daily assignments—but because I make it seem so simple doesn't mean it actually is. It usually takes a few years before you begin to find your "groove" in what you are teaching and when, allowing you to adjust your schedule as needed.

"I hate your class!"

This statement was short and to the point, and it almost made me walk out of my classroom and flee to a corporate job. A student, upset with a grade they earned on an essay, made it a point to stop my class and let everyone in the class know how they felt about me.

"That's fine, Ms. Oliver. Now if you could rejoin us for our class that would behoove you." The student reluctantly sat back down, but not before she mumbled some select expletives under her breath.

I continued to teach and while students were working independently, I decided I needed to have a meeting with Ms. Oliver, and then speak to her parents. Mrs. Oliver wasn't listening to me as I explained to her that expletives weren't appropriate, I decided to take things a step farther. That evening, I called her mother and decided to discuss her daughter's behavior in class.

Instead of being apologetic, I found that the mother of this child was just as verbally abusive. Within the first two minutes of the phone call, she had accused me not "liking" her child and giving her too much work. It was obvious that I was not going to get any further with her so I ended the call with a suggestion that the parent could meet with me at the school if she had any other concerns.

The next morning my student and her mother, Mrs. Oliver, were waiting for me in the front office. Sensing there was going to be a problem, my principal decided to sit in the conference. I explained (again) the child's lack of focus and obvious disrespect in my classroom. About a minute in, her mother decided that she was going to start to verbally abusing me once again.

I stopped the conference and turned to my principal. I told her that I did not have to put up with abuse when the child was at fault.

I thanked the parent for coming, gathered my things, and left the room.

On that day, I realized it was easy to get a job in the classroom. The hard part was going to be keeping it with clients like this.

10
So You Have Started Teaching— What's Next?

After you have planned everything you can, what comes next? Ideally, you would be ready to start educating children. The first day of school is always nerve-racking, but what happens after the kids have arrived and you have taught your first lesson? Realistically the first day (or even week) of school is full of imposters of your actual students. These imposters usually behave well and just sit and stare at you until they "read" what you expect in your classroom. For new teachers this time could literally be a day or week; it all depends on your class. Then comes the inevitable questions: Will the kids continue to be well behaved or will there come a time when you will have difficulties with both your job and the kids? Realistically, most teachers encounter problems as they find their teaching groove.

In my first year teaching, everything went fine—at first. The kids were still in "school mode" and they were trying to discover who I was as a teacher. But a month into the school year, I started to have trouble. I think the kids (especially the girls) realized I was young so they refused to listen to my instructions. In addition, I realized that being a teacher was very overwhelming and that I could not keep up with all I had to do: keeping my classroom organized, calling parents, writing lesson plans and then dealing with an ever-changing curriculum. Almost stressed to the point where I wanted to quit, I decided I had to have a plan if I was going to make it to the end of the year. Slowly, I began to observe veteran teachers and thought about what I could incorporate in my classroom to make my classroom run more efficiently.

After careful reflection, I quickly realized that my classroom was my business. In order for my business to succeed, I had to develop a mission statement and a plan to accomplish that mission. Luckily, by having that epiphany, I quickly regained control over my classroom. Instead of kids hating me for having strict rules, they all seemed to love the new structure. While I was able to turn my classroom environment around, other teachers are not that lucky.

Even in my thirteenth year of teaching, I can have the entire class running like a well-oiled machine, but it only takes one student to bring that machine to a grinding halt. I can distinctly remember one day teaching my heart out when there was a knock in the door. There was a student there with the counselor. She handed me his registration papers and informed me that Mark had been transferred to our school due to some type of incident at his last school. I didn't have time to learn about what happened so I let Mark in my room and then quickly went back to teaching my class.

After getting my kids to work independently, it was clear that Mark was used to doing his own thing. I made sure he understood to sit in his assigned seat, and I continued teaching. After a couple of days in the class, I began to hear whispers from the other students about what got Mark expelled from his last school. I kept hearing words such "gang fight," "assault on teacher," and other things, and I already knew things could get really bad—if I allowed it.

Since Mark was far more mature than the other students, I made it a point to have him as one of the leaders in the class. He helped pick up papers and run errands for me. He even managed to do work for me, when he was in school. Despite him being good for me, he was an absolute terror to the other teachers. He used his bigger size and his alleged criminal record to intimidate them in the classroom. I was designated as the teacher that would talk to him when he began to "smell himself." By the end of the semester (before he moved out of the district), Mark was a fully functioning student—all because I stayed on him. However, what about the new teachers in the building who seriously struggled to keep students like him engaged in class?

In addition to having increased classroom sizes, a new curriculum, and new teacher evaluation systems, many districts have all but eliminated support for new or inexperienced teachers. Some districts simply pair new teachers with veteran teachers, but this can be hit or miss. So what do teachers do? Just continue to have problems and hope someone from the front offices see your smoke signal for help? Of course not!

As you read, take a moment to reflect on where you are in the classroom. Are you excelling in some areas but struggling in other areas? Are you already burned out and it's only halfway into the year?

In this next section, I'm going to give teachers realistic, easy-to-implement strategies to help teachers confront problems they may encounter in their classroom.

Late one afternoon, I had to go back to my school because I left my telephone charger in my room. As I walked pass my colleague's door, I noticed he was at his desk, packing up his belongings. I peeked my head in.

"Hey, Mr. Z! Where are you going? Are you taking an early vacation?" I asked jokingly, but I was concerned that he seemed to really be going somewhere.

Startled by my voice, he turned around and looked me in the eyes. "I'm done. I can't take this anymore. I'm not returning."

Mr. Z was a first-year mathematics teacher who never seemed to be able to just teach. There were constant disruptions in his class and despite my attempts to help him, he wasn't prepared to work in an urban environment.

Knowing that Mr. Z was at his breaking point, I asked him what had pushed him over the ledge. He admitted that earlier that day he was observed by our principal and was marked down, despite his repeat requests for help in those areas. As I listened to him and heard the sheer defeat in his voice, I understood that Mr. Z wasn't a bad teacher. He was just lacking the tools to help him excel in his field.

Mr. Z was one of those teachers who could have been saved. Public school education needed him.

11

It's Normal To Be Overwhelmed

Before becoming a teacher, I never realized the sheer amount of paperwork we are responsible for on a daily basis. In between lesson plans, parent contact logs, grading papers, and filling out district paperwork, teachers literally go to bed having nightmares about what they need to do to get ahead. Even with the Internet, it seems as if the paper load for teachers is ever increasing. When teachers are accountable for everything, it is always good to think of yourself as the boss of the classroom and any good boss learns how to delegate.

While students are wonderful people to help with paperwork, realistically some of the paperwork can only be done by the teacher. So what can teachers do?

Stay organized

I always create a binder where I keep a contact sheet on every student I teach. The binder is arranged alphabetically and students have to fill out the contact sheet the first day of school (to ensure I get the correct information). Behind the sheet, I put assessment scores, progress reports and other important data on the kids. When I call parents, I have my binder ready and I document if I left a message, spoke to a parent, or if the phone number was not working. I even have a section that the students had to sign to acknowledge they saw their grades.

Having this data has protected me as a professional and really comes in handy during parent-teacher conferences. There have been plenty of times when parents have walked into conferences and swore they had no idea about their child's grades. I would simply show the documentation where I tried to contact a parent and where their child had signed to show I was doing my due diligence. This type of paperwork usually ends any dispute over what I am doing in my classroom. For younger grades, it is always good to keep a contact binder because again it protects you as a teacher and show that you are making contact with parents and guardians.

Practice good time management

I budget my time on what work I can get accomplished at school. My first two years of teaching I was teaching from 7:30 to 2:15 and working well into the night on lesson plans, contacting parents, etc. By the time January came around, I was drained. However, I decided that something had to change and the first thing I did was limit the amount of time I could spend outside of school on school affairs. Now rarely do I bring arbitrary work home. If I bring something home, it is super important and it is usually only once a week.

During the day, I made sure that every day during my planning period I had a goal of accomplishing some task that was on my to-do list. With only 55 to 90 minutes of planning, I would usually manage to grade papers for one class, create an assessment, or even contact parents. But every day I have a goal and I am only satisfied if I accomplished it. In addition, at night instead of lugging home stacks upon stacks of papers, I would only bring home something I could work on within my set time period (i.e. two hours). That way I never felt obligated to stay up to midnight to get everything graded.

When I used these methods, I found that by the end of the week the only thing I had left to do were lesson plans, not the 10 other things that I did during the week. Even during breaks, I employ this method of getting things done bit by bit. During the two weeks most teachers are out for winter break, I use that time to get caught up on grades, planning, and parent contact. So I allocate two hours a day to classroom duties. In the end, I go back to school relieved and without a load of work to do when I return.

Be aware of what you can (and cannot) finish on your time schedule

One of the usual complaints I hear from teachers is not being able to finish all 50 of the tasks you need to get done. Instead of trying to do all 50 tasks, focus on the most important and then finish accordingly. Teachers are not superheroes and often when we try to be, we are ready to quit by December. I can distinctly remember sitting at my desk between year three to five, and crying because I was overwhelmed. I was fed up with being asked to do everything. After feeling like blowing up, I decided that saying "no" was the quickest recipe for sanity.

My son had just started first grade and he was struggling with the curriculum. During the first round of progress reports, he had made an F. As I contemplated what to do, I decided the most immediate thing to do was to begin to say "no" and mean it. After having a talk with my principal, I politely declined being the head of the newly formed bowling team and all other extracurricular activities. While I fulfilled my duties of teaching the curriculum, I decided not to do anything extra that year.

By the end of the year, not only did my son end up doing really well, but I felt so refreshed. I followed that same mantra over the next few years and severely limited my extracurricular activities. My job is to teach and no matter how much I want to be the cheerleading coach, I have to remember my time (and sanity) is valuable.

Time management and organization are two skills that are highly needed in order to be an effective teacher. These skills are not easy to develop, but they're important so that you aren't burned out and ready to leave by December.

The running joke in my classroom is that it's not a 100% democracy, and at times it can be a dictatorship. Nothing is more evident than on the first day of class...

"Everyone line up in a straight line," I say. "Today is the first day of school and contrary to popular belief, we learn starting with day one. As soon as the bell rings, I expect for everyone to quietly walk in to the room and get your papers out to learn."

As soon as the bell rings, I hand out an infograph on the Trojan War and I begin teaching. The class was full of interesting facts about the war, and students see clips the classic play, "The Iliad." For the next ninety minutes, I demand my student's full attention. As soon as class is about to be over, I give my students their first assignment—write me a letter about who they are as a student, teenager and English student. By the time they leave, even the wildest student is in a state of shock—who teaches on the first day of school?

I always answer with a smile, "I do. Have a great day!"

For the past 13 years, this is how I have started my class. And every year I start the second day with everyone receiving my syllabus and me giving students a playbook on what is acceptable in my literature class. I rarely have discipline issues.

I'm the boss of my classroom.

12
Be The Boss Of Your Classroom

Every classroom has them and every teacher dreads them—the kids who come into class thinking that your classroom is their playground. Sometimes the kids are overt and do things without you knowing while other times they are "turned up" from the moment they enter your doors. They do things like mock you to the class, defy your orders, and hardly do any work.

In my career as a classroom teacher, I think I have managed to teach every knucklehead known to man and through those experiences I've figured out there are five types of students in any room.

Student A: This is the student who really wants to learn. They do exactly what you ask them to do, they always have their work, and they hang on your every word. Sometimes they come from great families but more times than not, they come from homes that are less structured but It does not matter who is doing what in the classroom, they are going to learn.

Student B: This is the student who is like student A in that they want to learn, but they cannot take any type of distraction. Once they are distracted, they do not regain focus on their work until the classroom is settled. Most students like this want to learn but due to a possible medical condition (like ADHD, autism, etc.) they have a hard time getting settled. Despite their issues paying attention, these students are never disrespectful or disruptive to the teacher.

Student C: This student is not only constantly disruptive but they never do any work. They are usually referred to as the class clown and they know how to get the entire class off track by either telling jokes (usually at other students' expense) or just being all over the place. They can rarely complete an assignment due to them always in trouble for disrupting the class. They do not have low skills across the board, but they have serious learning gaps.

Student D: This student is a serious behavior problem. Sometimes they have already been identified through special education as emotionally disturbed while other times they have moved around school so much no one has had time to evaluate them to see if they need additional services. They do not do any work because they lack the skills to be a student. They are violent with other students if provoked and have to be monitored constantly to make sure they are doing what they need to do.

Student E: This student rarely comes to class because of his/her many discipline infractions. If they do come to class, they're usually forced to attend. When they do come to your class they make it a point of doing something so serious they end up being put out, leaving the classroom in disarray. These kids are a danger to themselves and others.

You can get any of these types of students in your class. Some days classroom management is easy, while other days it can bring you to your knees. About five years ago, I happened to teach a class of first-time ninth graders who were all overage for the grade. The youngest student was 16 years old and to say that these students were a handful was an understatement. For every type of student listed above, I had at least five students from each category. My most memorable student was nicknamed "Goonie" and whenever a student said anything out of the way to me, she would lose her mind. Literally everyday was a juggling act of keeping the students calm, motivated, or out of lock up. These are the strategies I used to help me get through that year.

First, I adjusted my attitude. Every morning I tried to come in with a positive attitude, despite what the students did. This seems like a simple piece of advice but this is probably one of the most important things new teachers have to know. You have to go into your classroom like you are an expert—even if you do not yet believe it. That does not mean being a know-it-all, but instead going in with the confidence that you know more than your students and that you are there to give them some of that knowledge.

I remember specifically when I decided to teach summer school during my third year in the classroom. Summer school in this particular district was divided by grade levels and it was normal for students to fight and eventually be dismissed from summer school. I was teaching a class of juniors who had failed their American literature class during the regular school year. I was their only hope of becoming a senior the following year. I decided to test my strategies to ensure that students listened. As the summer started, students quickly realized that I looked young but I knew my content. We worked from the bell to the end of the day. At the end of the summer program, I had kids begging me to come to their school and be their regular teacher.

The second step with being a confident teacher is always keeping students engaged with quality work and activities. Ever since my first year as a teacher, I learned that if students were always learning, it was less likely they would act up. So I always had more things for kids to do. The smart kids (student A/B) I always tailor their work to make it a little bit more difficult so they would stay engaged.

For the kids who struggled (usually student C) I always tried to pair them up with a super serious student so they didn't have anyone to engage in their foolery. After a while, they would get tired and just figure if they got on task they'd be allowed to sit with their friends. Students who fit into the D/E category were strategically placed throughout the room to make sure that I could easily get to them if necessary.

My former student Mark (who was being forced to come to school by his parole officer) had moments where he was all five types of students. There were times when he'd be so engaged in a lesson that he'd want to fight other children if they disrupted the class. Then there were times he'd literally come into class and be so tired that he'd want to sleep the entire time. Depending on the type of student that showed up that day, that dictated how I would deal with him.

Seating charts

For some, seating charts seem like an archaic system to ensure that students were always where they needed to be. As a high school teacher, I rarely used them in some classes, but in other classes they were a literal lifesaver. The first week is a time for me to learn their personalities. I carefully watch and observe who may have vision problems, who is in which clique, and who needs to sit near me. After the first week, I explain I'm exercising my "executive power" and that everyone will have new seats. I then make my seating charts for the classes that need more structure.

When I taught ninth grade, they always needed seating charts due to immaturity and academic and behavioral issues. Seating charts allowed me to teach without the worry that students who were not supposed to sit with one another would somehow find one another while I was teaching.

In a rare case, there would be students who would flat out refuse to sit where you assign them. Then I would do the following: At the beginning of class, I would make all students line up outside the door, and give students a slip with their seat number. If a student has a problem where they are sitting, they can write me a note and I will quietly address it when the class is settled and make changes as needed. Seating charts are almost required when teaching elementary and middle school but in high school, teachers use them as necessary. You almost always need them with ninth graders; however, the higher you go, the less likely you will have to use them.

Expectations

From the moment students enter my class and I hand them my syllabus, students understand that I hold them to high expectations. They see it in what I wear, in how my classroom is set up, the amount of learning that occurs—basically everything I do. That's why I begin teaching immediately. Students are first confused and say things like, "It's the first day of school; we aren't supposed to do any work!" But as I move quickly, they begin to realize that work is indeed going to take place in my room. During that first month of school, I am quick to correct student's behaviors. For example, when I am teaching students cannot leave their seats. If a student happens to get up, I acknowledge that this is a classroom "no-no", direct the student back to their seat, and still continue to teach.

I make it a point never to interrupt learning to address a student's misbehavior. I redirect them, continue teaching, and then deal with the student in the hallway once the class can work independently. I also utilize parents a lot during that time. If a student is particularly disruptive, I like to call their parent often. It doesn't matter if they respond or not, just the sheer fact that I'm "bugging" them will make them address the issue eventually. In addition, I like students to think that there's nothing I wouldn't do to make my classroom run smoothly. During my planning period, I might call a parent and invite them up to the school. Even with the most disengaged parent, I've learned that they are appalled when they learn their child is acting up at the beginning of the school year. I've even had parents tell me that they were "highly annoyed" when I continually call them. That is fine by me as long as they made sure that their child behaved.

Any student who walks into my classroom understands that my classroom is my world. I build the class culture by making it seem like learning is the most important thing going on in the classroom. If there's a disruption in class due to misbehavior, I always point out to the kids that this is impeding our class time and ask what they think is the appropriate punishment.

Despite all of the safeguards put in place to ensure students do not act up, they do. Some do not care if you call their parents or call the principal so what do you do? Document every negative interaction with that child and document the results. Many times students don't realize how misbehavior can really affect their grades. With these students, I always had plenty of meetings with the parents (if I could get a hold of them), the school counselor, the school social worker and other concerned adults in the classroom. Usually by the end of the first semester, students realized that they would get tired before I did and they decided that it was in their best interest to calm down and "act right." By the end of the year, some students had completely turned over a new leaf and for that we were all grateful.

Early in my career, I'd lose sleep that a child was misbehaving. But as I matured as a teacher, I have put in place so many strategies that rarely do I have a student who purposely misbehaves.

At the beginning of the year, I give my expectations and consequences and I follow them. Remember you are the adult. You are the boss of your classroom.

One afternoon as I was returning from eating my lunch outside, I saw one of my parents walking toward me in the hallway.

"Ms. Warren, have you seen Terrence today?" she asked me before I could say hello.

"Um, yes, He was in my second period class, but I haven't seen him since then," I replied.

At that moment, Terrence came around the corner, with a bag from the local fast food restaurant and holding his girlfriend's hand.

I knew that things were going to go bad—fast.

Before I could say anything else, his mother charged toward him. "Where have you been in my car? I went to the student parking lot and I didn't see it."

"Um, I was just…" Terrence tried to tell her where he had been but before he could get it out his Mom yelled again.

"Don't lie! Once I realized my car wasn't in the parking lot, I had your Aunt drive to around to McDonalds and why did I see you and her"—pointing at his girlfriend—"in my car, off campus with her driving!"

By this time, other students had gathered to watch Terrence's mother berate him. His girlfriend, sensing things were going to go bad quickly, was slowly backing up to get out of reach of Ms. Jones' hand.

"Mom! No, you didn't! We…" Before he could get anything else out, his mom lunged at him.

I quickly dropped my stuff and grabbed his mother. By this time a male teacher had noticed the fracas, grabbed Terrence, and put him in his room. Our principal came and cleared the hallway.

After everything was calm, my co-workers and I had a quiet laugh. What possessed students to do crazy things when they knew they were going to get caught?

13
It's Okay To Laugh, Right?

It never fails that students do things that will have you laughing so hard that you find yourself crying. Sometimes these instances happen unexpectedly while other times they are carefully orchestrated fiascos.

During my first year of teaching, I was lucky enough to have a phone in my classroom. I used it to not only contact parents, but it was convenient to have a number where people could get in contact with me if something was wrong with my son. About three months into school, someone kept calling the phone and breathing heavily on the other line. At first, I chalked it up to someone with the wrong number, but after about three calls in one day, I knew that it was obviously someone pranking me.

Not wanting to disturb my students by yelling into the phone, I decided that the next time someone called, I would simply leave the phone off the hook. Just like clockwork, the phone rang and I noticed that this time the caller began to breathe very heavily. As I was listening, I happened to turn around and notice my class prankster, Branden, was laughing uncontrollably. As a matter of fact, most of the class was snickering. I didn't want them to know I saw them so instead of leaving the phone on, I decided to hang up. I then went over to my student files and looked up Branden's cell phone number. As the kids had their back to me, I decided to call his number.

    As I suspected, when the phone rang I saw Branden* look at his lap. He was the person prank calling me. I quietly called him to the back of the classroom and before I could say anything, he started laughing. I simply shook my head and held my hand out. As he handed over the phone I scolded him at his immaturity and later on handed the phone over to our assistant principal as I chuckled and told her what happened.

    As a teacher, it is easy to lose your sense of humor when you are trying to get through a lesson. However, taking the time to have a laugh can help you release some pent up stress while being in the classroom. This was evident one time during my second year of teaching as I was teaching my students the importance of the Harlem Renaissance to American Literature. As students were reading excerpts from Zora Neale Hurston's *Their Eyes*

Were Watching God, one of my students, Lily, had fallen asleep while reading her assigned section.

Before I could say anything, another student decided to take their textbook and slam it on the ground beside her. Just at that moment, Lily jumped up out of her seat and yelled, "They're shooting! Everyone duck!" We were too stunned to say anything and when Lily realized we were still in class, she started laughing and so did we. After laughing for a couple of minutes, we went back to *Their Eyes Were Watching God* and Lily stayed awake for the rest of class.

While the majority of the time it's students who make you laugh during the day, sometimes your parents can bring you the most joy. About four years into my time in the classroom, my mentor teacher came and saw me after class. Apparently she had called a parent that morning about their son, Ronny, acting up in the class. After speaking with the parent, the teacher realized that the parent was a disciplinarian and promised her that should no longer have any issues in the classroom with him. My mentor teacher went back to teaching and about an hour later, Ronny was in her class when he got called out for a visitor in the hallway. About two minutes into Ronny leaving the classroom, she began to hear a woman shouting. The women's voice was steadily getting louder and louder and before long, the teacher peeked her head in the hallway. There was Ronny's mother in the hallway, with a belt about to spank Ronny for him misbehaving. Mortified, the mentor teacher ran out in the hallway and intervened, but not before the parent let everyone in the hallway know what would happen to Ronny when he got home. Needless to say the parent left and Ronny came back to class a completely different person. As she told me this story, I could hardly contain myself—especially when Ronny attempted to act up in the classroom. For the rest of the year there was no need for teachers to bring up what happened to Ronny, his classmates made his mother almost spanking him in the hallway the running joke.

These moments of silliness are nice class refreshers to not only students, but also to teachers. After all, it is okay to laugh, right?

"I don't know what it is. I just hate to call parents. They're always so…unpredictable."

This was part of a conversation that I had with a co-worker about why she absolutely hated to call parents about anything good or bad. She reasoned with me that one time she'd called a parent about a child's failing grade, and the parent had threatened to beat her ass if she called her one more time. Needless to say, I helped her make phone calls.

Over the past 13 years, I've probably called thousands of parents and each time someone picks up, you never know what you're going to hear. I've heard:

"The next time you call my house I'm going to come up there and meet you. You always keep me so informed about what is going on."

"Honestly, we can't do anything with him at home. Tell me if anything you guys do works for him."

"That's my baby—she would never use that type of profanity."

"The last I checked I dropped them off at school. Aren't they ya'll's problem now?"

"I didn't think kids still got suspended for fighting. Isn't that normal behavior?"

"The next time you call me, I'm changing my number."

14
Communication Is A Necessary Evil

It never fails that every year I call a parent and get cursed out. Sometimes it's not intentional (they're stressed out about their job or I call at a bad time), but other times my ear becomes the whipping stick just because. I used to get really upset, but now when I encounter this type of parent, I simply let it roll off my back. However, communication with parents can be a very complex area of our job.

Every teacher has so much loaded on their plates that communicating with parents is the last thing they want to do. Combine that with the fact that parents can get hostile when they get bad news about their child's academic progress and sometimes teachers will avoid contact like the plague. However, it is a necessary evil. There's no excuse for not trying to contact a parent.

In this new day and age, the traditional phone call may not be the best way to contact a parent. Some parents work nontraditional shifts or jobs. Some work at night and sleep during the day. I've even had some parents who are truck drivers. They're gone for several weeks at a time so I had to figure out how to contact them. Be creative and use these new communication tips to make your job easier.

Parent newsletter

This is one of the things that elementary schools do very well. Using programs like Microsoft Publisher, you can create a newsletter in a couple of clicks. Use this platform to convey messages to parents: supplies needed for the classroom, important dates to remember, and information on what students are doing in the classroom. There is no cost to teachers, and it should be easy to go into the office to print.

While it would be ideal to produce a newsletter once a week, it may be difficult to maintain that frequency. Every two weeks may be a better time period. Whenever I would send my newsletters out, I would get help from students who either needed community service hours or who were good writers to help me get the newsletter written up.

E-mail

You will always have a good number of your parents who are more likely to check their e-mail than to answer a phone call. At the beginning of the year when both parents and students are more likely to give me their correct contact information, I always ask for e-mail addresses. Whenever I call a parent and there's no answer, I always follow up with a standard e-mail. This is a good way to show documentation that you have indeed contacted parents. Frankly, it is easier to type a quick e-mail than to constantly call a parent who you already know is not going to call you back. It also is a good way to keep parents informed without them having to come up to the school on a constant basis.

Classroom blog

From projects, to service learning opportunities, to supply requests, a blog is your answer. Having a blog is basically free for educators with sites like Edmodo, Wordpress, Blogger, and Wikispaces. A classroom blog is a great way to keep parents informed of everything that's happening in the classroom.

Social media (Twitter, Facebook, etc.)

Almost everybody is on social media today. If you create a Twitter or Facebook page for your class, you can update your parents and students without ever having to see their social media profiles. Make sure the privacy settings are set to "open" so that students are not required to be your friend to get updates. Then get to updating!

Online grading books

This is a powerful tool to keep parents informed about the child's progress. Sites like SnapGrades, MyGradeBook, and many others give teachers easy interfaces to update grades with the click of a mouse. These sites are reasonably priced and are wonderful because each student gets individual log-ins for themselves and their parents.

Parent conferences

While this is an age-old communication strategy, it is one of the most effective. The problem is actually getting parents to come to them. In efforts to schedule conferences that parents can attend, I usually have one day a week where parents can come and meet with me (after school or during my planning period) to discuss grades, behavior, and accomplishments of their children. In addition, I also make sure that conferences are highly structured. I always try to start with positives in the class and with the student, then I discuss issues that may be a challenge. I always try to focus on behavior, not the student. In the end, we usually realize the changes that need to occur.

In the event that parents want to be contacted, the above measures are all great tools to protect what you do in the classroom. However, here's something many teachers don't know until they get into the classroom: there are parents out there who don't want to have any contact with the teachers. I've had students who've sat in my class all year and despite my endless attempts, I can't get in contact with the parents. To protect myself, I always make students sign that they received progress reports, and attended (or did not attend) tutorial. I keep call logs from attempted parent attempts to ensure that at the end of the year they don't show up and swear I didn't contact them. If it's an urgent request to speak to a parent, I usually contact the school's social worker and allow them to work their magic to get in contact with someone in the household.

In the past 13 years, I have only not been able to contact about five parents. Remember parent communication is key.

> During my third year of teaching, I learned a valuable lesson. My son was in first grade and during the first nine weeks, he was struggling with the content. As I received his progress report, all I saw were Cs, Ds, and Fs. I was devastated.
>
> Short of becoming a crazed parent, I went to meet with his teacher, Ms. Boyd, who had happened to have taught first grade for the last 30 years. To say she was intimidating was an understatement. As I asked her about what else I could do to help him with the content, she said in her no nonsense tone, "Teach him to read. If he can't read, I can't pass him."
>
> The only way that I could do to help him was to excuse myself from all the extracurricular activities that I was involved in.
>
> The next morning, I went to my principal and told her that I could no longer stay longer than an hour after school and I could only hold tutorials on Saturday mornings.
>
> She agreed.
>
> For the next six months, I worked with my son on his reading and math. By the end of the year, he was able to master the first grade standards. From then on, I vowed that I would no longer devote all my time to school. My family needed me.
>
> I didn't have to live at the school. I could just do my job, go home, and still be a good teacher.

15

Do Your Job!

As a teacher, this seems like a simple concept but it is something that has to be said. As teachers, we are called to be a sponsor for clubs, help with community organizations, help with the school play, coach a sport and even sometimes act as a chauffeur for students. In the midst of doing all of these other jobs, it is easy to forget what your main job is—teaching students.

As a new teacher, I was doing so much extra stuff that sometimes I was pulled away from my job of teaching students. There were days where I was coaching bowling and didn't get home until late at night after games. With a small child and husband at home, I was seriously neglecting them. Reality slapped me in the face, when I got my son's first report card in first grade. It was full of Ds and Fs. I knew he was struggling and I had gone to the school to meet with the teacher and come up with strategies to help him. But I was still shocked when I saw his grades. At that moment, I realized that I needed to spend more time with him.

As I realized this, I really had to take account on why I was a teacher, which was to make a difference in student's lives. While I could be a great coach and club sponsor, the best change I could make was to be a phenomenal classroom teacher and mother.

Upon realizing that I could not do everything, I had to step back and excuse myself from activities that interfered with my job as a teacher and my job as a mother.

After finding out my son was struggling in first grade, I walked into my principal's office and told her I had to take some time off after school. Being a mother herself, she understood and we agreed that I could hold my tutorial on Saturday mornings and that I could only stay one hour after school for tutorial. The more I began to free myself from the "extras," the more time I had to devote to myself as a professional and to my family.

There were some days that I had to learn how to be okay with leaving work immediately after school and not staying for hours trying to get caught up in paperwork. I even started carefully monitoring how I spent my time during my planning period so I could be as productive as possible. I made a goal to accomplish at least one thing each day. My goal could range from grading a classroom set of essays to calling parents. Whatever the goal was, I was determined to finish it so that I could be free to be a more productive professional and person.

Have a life outside of school

It is common for students to think that teachers have no lives outside of school. The stark reality is that often we don't spend time outside of school on ourselves. By year five of my teaching career, my life consisted of teaching, playing with my son, and then going to bed. I was burned out. I had stopped making sure that I was okay. I think I realized it when I walked past the mirror and did not realize who I was anymore. I had gained 25 pounds and I was a shell of the person I had once been.

In order to get back to a sense of "self" I decide to take up running, but for you it may be something completely different. Take a moment and think about what you love to do and do it. Don't feel guilty about having a life outside of school. Remember to be discreet, however, if what you like to do may get you "called on the carpet" at your school.

The only way you can be a happy teacher is to take care of yourself. Teaching may be a selfless job, but that does not mean you have to sacrifice your sanity or family to be a good teacher. I make sure that I take time for myself by running and spending time with my family. Even now after being in the classroom for 13 years, I always remember to put myself first.

> *"I swear everyday there's someone new in my room. Sometimes it's our principal or instructional coach, then other times it's my mentor, then sometimes it's even someone from the district office! When will they leave and just let me teach?"*
>
> *This was my eleventh year in the classroom and I was trying to give my newest co-worker some advice. The sheer amount of people entering her room was mind-blowing. As someone who had experienced the same thing, I understand her pain because as a new teacher I constantly received visitors in my classroom.*
>
> *As I finished listening to her talk, I said, "You know what you should do? Just close your door and teach."*

16

They Won't Leave My Room!

As a new teacher, I can remember having numerous people (from my school and the district) observe my teaching. They would come in as quiet as they could with their clipboards in hand, nodding their heads with questioning looks. Sometimes they would stay an entire period, while other times they were only there for five minutes. Sometimes while my kids were working, they would come and kneel by them and quietly ask them about their work, while other times they would just sit in the back of the classroom and just watch me.

While it's annoying, it is inevitable that as a new teacher people will be in your classroom—all the time. Sometimes administrators come in to see if you are actually teaching, while other times an instructional coach may come in to help you with an area of growth. Other times parents come in to "check on" their child, and other times people come just to… come.

As a new teacher, it is intimidating to have people come in and grade you for a snapshot of your classroom. When they enter, you want to stop the class and yell, "Leave me alone!" but you ultimately know that this is part of the job. Despite the jitters, this is a part of the job that never ends. If you are a teacher that needs development, people are going to visit your room and if you're a good teacher, they are still going to come. The best thing you can do is structure your class so that students know how to work if someone enters your classroom.

At the beginning of the year, I let all of my students know:

1. They may see strange adults in my classroom. It's okay. Act the same as before.
2. Model appropriate behavior from the first day of class onwards.
3. Act the same when people come and visit me as when they are not here.

Despite preparing my students for the visitors, at times the visits became overwhelming as a first-year teacher. I was rarely told what they were looking for, just what I was doing wrong. After my second year, I decided that I needed boundaries for people coming into my room. As I became a more seasoned teacher and even switched districts I made sure my boundaries in my classroom were clear to anyone entering the room. When visitors came to my room, I asked them to:

1. Come in three persons at a time.
2. Refrain from disrupt the students unless I gave previous permission.

3. Hold all questions until the end of class.

These boundaries help me maintain my class integrity and my sanity. In spite of all the safeguards I put in place, there was always a student who was enamored with our guests. I've had students completely stop working and watch the guests as they circled the room. One time I had a student tell a visitor they spoke "funny" (they were from the United Kingdom) when they asked him a question! Luckily, the visitor just laughed it off, but with teenagers, anything is possible.

There was one time in particular when someone from my district came in to film my class for a documentary they had going on about teachers in the district. While my kids were fine when the videographer came in, they lost their mind when he brought in all of his audiovisual equipment. Students literally stopped working and began to ask to the man to please let them talk on camera. Embarrassed, I had to ask the man to step out of the room and I gave the students a verbal lashing. When he re-entered the classroom, the students were calmer, but they couldn't help themselves from staring into the camera at times. I chuckled, but I knew there was little I could do to stop it and I just continued to teach.

I always let my students know that despite visitors are in my room, I will remain the same. So if a student says something out of line, I usually will pull that student to the side during independent work and let them know that's not acceptable behavior.

Even now, I still have people in my classroom, but it's not for the same reasons as my first year of teaching- now it's to help teachers perfect their craft.

> *"Ms. Warren! Hurry! She's in the hospital! She's hurt really bad!"*
>
> *I received this phone call late one Saturday night from one of my students who spent a lot of time with me outside the classroom.*
>
> *Scared, I quickly jumped up, threw on some clothes, and rushed down to the downtown trauma hospital in Memphis, The Med.*
>
> *As soon as I entered, I was met by my student's father. He said one of the worst things I had ever heard: "There's been a bad accident. They're going to have to operate."*
>
> *I just sat in the chair with the family and thought, "Why do bad things happen to good kids?"*

17

When Bad Things Happen To Kids

During my time in the classroom, I have seen everything—good, bad and ugly—happen to the kids who enter my room every day. I have had students killed in bad accidents, raped, taken away from their parents, and even put in jail. Every tragic situation is different, but what I have learned through it all is that bad things sometimes happen to kids and as an educator, I have to acknowledge that.

The first time I experienced tragedy was when one of my students was in a horrible car accident. She had extensive injuries and had to have numerous surgeries, but she survived. As she recovered, I was sure to allow the kids who were in her class the opportunity to talk about the accident and their fears. While I thought the experience of seeing a student battered and bruised up was bad, nothing prepared me for the death of a student my fourth year in the classroom.

In 2006, a particularly well liked student of mine was killed in a car crash. As all car crashes are it was sudden and despite no one believing it was serious the student died from internal bleeding soon after arriving at the hospital. To say that this student's death was a shock was an understatement. The next day, I awoke to hundreds of text messages informing me of the accident and students coming up to the school (it was summer school) crying and despondent. How could such a smart student lose their life through no fault of their own?

What made her death so bad for the teachers in the building was that she had millions of dollars in scholarships and was just a genuinely good student. When I initially found out the news, I was in shock and did not believe it. However, when all of the kids met at the school in the following days, I knew it was real. Instead of trying to be strong, I cried with the kids and hugged them. During the funeral, it was so humbling to see students just so devastated at her death. For a long time it was hard for me to come to terms with her death and I just couldn't understand why something so bad would happen to such a good kid.

Being a teacher allows you to witness many things that have the capacity to go wrong for students. I've witnessed students have horrible things happen to them just from the household they were born in. There have been times that because a student shared an experience with me, I've had no choice but to contact our school social worker.

    I can remember one time in particular, when I questioned a student who missed multiple days of school every week. After questioning him, he confessed that his mother was forcing him to stay at home and watch his siblings and that was why he missed so much school. I sympathized with this student because he wanted to be loyal to his mother, but his loyalty was costing him his education. After talking with him for hours, I sent him to the school social worker, but I went home with a heavy heart that night and wondered, "Why do bad things happen to kids?"

    After those varying experiences, I learned that sometimes bad things happen to the kids who come in your room. Whenever something happens, it helps to express how I feel with the other students and pray for some type of peace for the family of the student. As a teacher, it's our job to be compassionate and let the kids express their feelings. It's hard, but it's a lesson I learned through the pain.

> *"Principal. No. Assistant Principal. No. Guidance counselor. No. What am I supposed to do—teach for the rest of my life?!"*
>
> *These were my thoughts as I entered my sixth year of teaching and I started to think about what I would do next. As I searched the job board and PhD programs, I noticed that there didn't seem to be much of a career path for teachers. Either you teach for 35 years or you become a principal.*
>
> *As I researched more opportunities, I realized that professional opportunities were virtually nonexistent. That same year, as I was already thinking of making a transition, I was notified that due to budget restrictions, I was going being forced to reapply for my current teaching position due to a reduction in force.*
>
> *The time was now for me to make my brand.*

18

How To Create Your Own Professional Development

After teaching for a number of years the question then becomes how can you perfect your teaching craft? Should you return to graduate school or will you naturally became an expert after time in the classroom? At about year five I wanted to do something more with my teaching craft. I felt like I could not teach for the next 25 years doing the same thing year after year, so from that point on I decided I needed to perfect my craft.

Teaching has grown since compulsory education was introduced late 19th century. For decades, teachers have merely been thought of as employees of their respective school districts and were subject to their district's feeble attempts to give them professional development. But with the Great Recession in 2008, finding a teaching job has become harder. It's crucial for teachers to develop their own professional development that's not dependent on their district's model. While this may seem like a daunting task, it is easier if you are strategic.

I found out what happens if you just wait on the school district to lead your development. Despite the supposed job security of being a teacher (everyone has to educated in some capacity, right?), my job was not secure. After teaching for almost 12 years, I received notice that there was going to be a reduction in force. Basically, that meant that all content areas would lose teachers. As humiliating as it was, I was forced to reapply for my position in line with other professionals with PhDs, master's, and years of experience. In the end, I kept my job but several of my colleagues did not.

As I watched teachers struggle with possible unemployment, I realized that if I wanted to stay in education, I had to take control of my career. Yes, I work for a district, but that did not mean I should be dependent on them for my livelihood. I began to examine how lawyers and physicians were able to keep their livelihood by branding themselves. I knew I had to start thinking differently, unlike anything I was taught in both undergraduate and graduate school. It was time for me to begin to build my brand.

As I began to think about my strategy for branding, I looked at the resources I already had at my disposal. I realized that I constantly received flyers, emails, and letters about free professional development offered either through my district or another teacher organization. Like many of my colleagues, I never even thought about attending. I blamed my extensive master's program, but in reality, I was just being lazy. After I moved districts and I had a little bit more time, I decided to start to look into these opportunities and I found that some of the professional developments were great ways for me to perfect my craft! I started to attend select professional development offered by my district and even able to find free opportunities for teachers through the summer months. The more I attended these opportunities, the more I had a chance to speak to other teachers and network with other professionals in my content area.

Throughout this section, you will learn some strategies to take you from a fresh-eyed, bushy-tailed new teacher to a content specialist ready to change the classrooms across America.

> "Do you know what the kids say about you, Ms. Warren?" a student asked me after class one day.
>
> I responded with caution as I began to clean off my desk. "Unfortunately, I don't have my ear to the streets, Tina, but I'm sure I don't want to hear it."
>
> "No, it's good, Ms. Lane. All the kids say that you can teach your butt off and that you don't take any mess! See you tomorrow!" And just like that, Tina bounced out of my room. I smiled at her compliment as I cleaned up my room.
>
> From the time I was a third-year teacher, I had begun to hear whispers among the kids about me as a teacher. It was interesting to hear kids use adjectives like hard, mean, dedicated, loving, and caring to describe me.
>
> Little did I know that they way kids view you, is often the very beginning of building your brand.

19

You Are A Brand—Act Like It!

When you walk into any school, it is easy to find out who the most effective teachers are—just ask around. The students will point you to their direction, and other teachers will applaud their teaching skills. Kids seem to gravitate toward them. When asked what makes that teacher effective, people will reply it is their content area, their teaching strategies, their enthusiasm for the students, and their abilities to help students achieve. Essentially, their abilities, enthusiasm and strategies are that teacher's brand.

    According to TheEducatorsRoom.com, (a site I created after almost being laid off) a teacher's brand is the type of product (strategies, content, delivery, pedagogy) that a teacher consistently delivers under their name. For many teachers, this is a new concept. Their skills are not only meaningful but can be thought of as a brand like Apple or Microsoft.

When you view your skills as a brand, it allows you to not be at mercy of the respective districts they work for. With job cuts becoming more and more common, excellent teachers are finding themselves without employment or terribly underemployed. They have nothing but their degrees and no classroom to use them in. So what can teachers do to protect their livelihoods?

Treat your teaching career like a brand

Before I go any further, think about the well-known educators that we see on our nightly news and in magazines discussing issues that affect education. What really separates you from them? Maybe they've been the classroom longer? There are people who barely have three years of classroom experience making major decisions about what happens in education, so that can't be the case. Maybe they have a doctorate or master's that you don't have? Probably not. Mainly what separates them is that they view themselves as an expert, not merely a teacher who "just teaches."

These professionals have taken their content area and elevated themselves as the experts in the field. Often they begin their career as a wide-eyed teacher and then turn their experience into books, strategies, and even curriculum. Viewing yourself as an expert will allow you to change the way you view conferences and professional development/career advancement opportunities because instead of viewing them as "work" they are now necessary to take you into the expert category.

Keeping this in mind, everything you do as a professional should contribute to your teaching brand. Your brand should be so recognizable that if you were laid off, your name alone would make you employable. A good way to determine what your area of expertise is to take an objective look at your talent in the classroom then ask others (your students, parents, and colleagues) to determine your strongest area. From that feedback, start brainstorming what you could do with your area of expertise.

I can distinctly remember working with a chemistry teacher who had a doctorate, but she was convinced that all she could do was teach. She was a phenomenal teacher but due to all the mental abuse she received from our supervisor and students she had began to doubt her own talents. We decided to have her students and fellow peers take a quick, two-minute online survey about her strong areas in class management, assessment, and instruction. When she received the results, she was shocked to see that despite feeling the opposite, everyone viewed her as an expert. Armed with this confidence she decided to invest in herself. Before the next year, she was not only presenting at conferences, but she received an offer to train other scientists at an area chemical factory.

Whenever I speak about teacher branding, the question always comes up how to do it with the limited time/funds teachers have. It's simple.

You are likely already doing it but you just need some purpose to elevate what you're already doing. Many times the creating, honing, and practicing we already do for our job is our starting point and everything else will help you elevate your brand. In order to build your brand, you should do the following:

Make it a point to become an expert in your content level(s)

Once we get our degrees and take our courses to keep our teaching certificates, many of us never think to become even more educated in our content area(s). Take time now to take classes at the local university or community college in your content or in overall education classes. Apply for fellowships that will put you in an environment where you are always learning something new. Take time during the summer when you're off to "shadow" someone whose doing what you want to do in education. The point is use every chance you get to perfect your craft. For beginners this may feel uncomfortable, but remember that growth is supposed to be uncomfortable.

For example, once realizing that teachers needed help in their knowledge about special education, a former colleague decided to use YouTube to hold professional development for other teachers. She was the expert in special education and she took the initiative to highlight what she knew.

Attend professional development opportunities locally and nationally

Take a minute and look through your district's professional development book. If you see any events that interest you, attend. Also, look through other organizations for good professional development opportunities. Search the Internet for great (free) conferences such as Ed Camp or go to your local college and see what's presented at the local teaching conference.

As someone who works in a school 180 days of the year, the last thing most teachers want to do is to attend a professional development that isn't worth that paper it's advertised on. Early in my career, I only went to professional development events mandated by my principal. However, I learned that there are good professional development opportunities offered. You just have to search for it.

Join professional organizations

So many times teachers refuse to spend the extra money to become a member of the National Council of English Teachers, or National Council of Math Educators, etc. These are wonderful organizations to not only meet people in your content but to network with people who can let you know about wonderful opportunities. In addition to the great networking opportunities through national conferences, you also get first-hand access to printed materials such as magazines, scholarly journals, and more that can help you elevate your knowledge of the content.

Every professional organization puts on a national conference. What better way to increase your knowledge and still gain great professional insight than to join your national, state, and local professional organizations.

Present on your expertise

Many school leaders would love for teachers to take the initiative and lead training. We all understand that most faculty meetings are boring. Why not spice things up a bit and ask to lead training in an area that you're good in? The best faculty meeting I can remember is when a fellow teacher presented on a topic we cared about and showed us how we could solve problems in our school. Every educational conference has a call for submissions and this is a great time to get experience presenting at a national stage. It looks great on your resume to have presented on your ideals to a national audience.

Get published in educational magazines, journals, and/or articles about your expertise

When I started The Educator's Room, I wanted a place where the true experts—practicing teachers—could not only share their expertise, but could build their brands. Take time to research sites that will allow you to write articles and pitch ideas to them. (The Educator's Room is always looking for writers!)

Branding yourself is difficult; however, in these times it's crucial to your professional livelihood. The more that you build yourself up professionally, the less likely you will have to depend on a school district to protect you.

> "Where is it? Why is it every time I need it, I can't find it! This means that I'm going have to do it all over again! Grr!" I screamed as I hurriedly searched for my updated resume to apply for my "dream job" that was just posted on my school system's job board.
>
> After searching for 30 minutes, I realized that I couldn't find any version of my resume anywhere on my computer. So instead of spending the evening reading my new book or writing, I was up well past midnight attempting to re-create my resume.
>
> As I worked, a friend of mine texted me: "If you stay ready, you don't have to get ready."
>
> Lesson learned.

20

Keep Your Resume Updated

After I worked in my first school for a couple of years, I could not even find my resume, much less sit down and actually update it whenever I wanted to apply for a promotion. It was not until I was transitioning between school districts when I actually realized all of the work I did in my five years in my first school district. The problem was that when I was updating my resume I forgot numerous things I had been part of and had received accolades for. In five years, I had served on almost every committee at the school, had coached several sports, and had even presented at national conferences for my school! Imagine the nightmare it was for me to sit and remember everything of importance I had done while at that school!

As teachers, we do many extra things that can quickly be forgotten if we don't write it down. So every month, I recommend that teachers keep track of all the professional opportunities they've participated in and update their resume. This helps when a new position pops up at a moment's notice—you'll already have an updated resume. Once a year, I actually revise my entire resume while thinking about the following questions:

- What do I do daily in my classroom?
- What have I accomplished this year?
- What new trainings have I attended and/or lead?
- Have I been asked by my principal/district to do that's out of the ordinary?

At this point in my career, I actively look for opportunities to make me better as an educator, so instead of passing my resume around for random jobs, I've even become more strategic with my job hunting. About a year ago, I was introduced to the networking site, LinkedIn, by a mentor of mine. It's basically a platform where you can not only apply for jobs, but meet like-minded professionals.

Being on LinkedIn, I have been able to connect with so many opportunities that I would have never known about in the past. It's allowed me to have my resume on a platform where I can direct people to and update instantly with any accomplishments. In addition, I never have moments anymore where I can't find my resume!

> *For years I rolled my eyes at any type of professional development my district offered. When I was forced to attend a one, I was the one sitting in the back, planning how I could make the quickest exit at the end of the session.*
>
> *During year seven, I had an epiphany.*
>
> *I wanted to enjoy professional development, so I needed to find opportunities to lead them. I started small by asking my principal if I could present during in-service and/or during faculty meetings. With the positive feedback my co-workers gave me, I was encouraged to apply to present at district wide professional development.*
>
> *Now instead of hiding in the corner, I'm the person leading the professional development.*

21

If You Don't Want To Teach Until Retirement

Contrary to popular belief, being a teacher does not mean you have to be in the classroom for 35 years nor is your only career path to be a principal. There are countless opportunities for educators to move up (or out) of the classroom, if you are ready. Once teachers have been in the classroom for an extended amount of time, naturally you have the feelings that you may want to do something different while still helping students. I was no different. By year five, I wanted to do something different, but it didn't mean I was necessarily ready to leave my students. So in preparation for what I knew I would eventually do, I began to research opportunities to advance my career.

When I announced this to my friends who were teachers, some believed if you want to leave the classroom, you're a traitor to the kids. I absolutely do not believe that. Instead, I believe that sometimes teachers need to change up their path every five to ten years to stay fresh in the classroom. There are some teachers opt to stay in the classroom until they retire and I commend their dedication. However, if someone decides after a certain amount of years of teaching that they want to pursue another profession, that's totally acceptable.

When you realize your time is up in the classroom, what do you do? Do you have to become a principal or assistant principal or are there other careers you can transition into? Unbeknown to most, your degree in education is marketable. You just have to know where to look.

After teaching for 10 years, I was suddenly at risk for losing my job due to a "reduction in force" by the school district I was employed in. All of a sudden, having my livelihood threatened made me get out into the job force and see what was out there for someone who was an expert in education but lacked any corporate experience. For months, I spoke to friends who work in human resources and other teachers who left the profession and I actually got a promising list of what jobs are available for educators. Here are just a few jobs that many educators can transition to:

- Education consultant
- Communications expert/Writer/Book consultant
- Mathematician
- Corporate trainer

Looking at the job market is always hard. That's why it's always important to know the type of jobs that you qualify for. Many teachers can grasp that teaching is hard and sometimes everyone is not meant to be a teacher their entire life. If that time ever comes, it's smart to be prepared.

In addition to looking at traditional jobs like above, there are other opportunities to still teach and advance your career. I have several friends who decided to take their talents and teach overseas or for the Department of Defense who love it. Not only do they get to stay in the classroom, but teaching overseas many times affords them a more competitive salary and their living costs are paid by their employer. To make things even better, they have found that teaching (in other countries) is actually revered. Professionally teachers are held in the same esteem as physicians so the morale among teachers is much better!

Regardless of the path you take (traditional vs. nontraditional) it's always important to look for opportunities where you can still use your skills you've developed while in the classroom. Teaching is one of the world's hardest professions in the world and thankfully, it can prepare you for any position.

"Don't leave us! We'll miss you!" My students exclaimed as I broke the news that I would be transferring from my job in the classroom to work closer with new teachers. Students were extremely emotional and seeing them get upset made me cry. As I wiped away my tears, I began to put into words the love and respect I had for all of them.

"When I started teaching I never thought that I would grow to love my students as much as I do. I can't wait to see you guys in college, raising your family and experiencing the highs and lows of working of adulthood." As I said those last words to them, my voice broke and the tears came.

At that moment one of my students hollered from the back of them room. "We love you also and don't ever forget about us because we'll never forget about you! Now lets talk about who is going to replace you because I need to get these credits!"

With that, the class exploded in laughter and all of a sudden I felt better. Better to take a chance on my career and leave the classroom a better person than when I entered it.

As I packed up my books two weeks later, I looked around the room where I spent the last 1,980 days of my life.

Teaching changed my life. I had survived behind the desk.

22

Joy Comes In The End

Up until three months ago, I was in the classroom still working with students, making sure I was changing students' lives. Then just like that, I was given the awesome opportunity to work more closely with new teachers. When I was first offered the job, I was torn on if I would actually take the new opportunity. For so long I had the opportunity to share the good, bad, and ugly with my students that I wondered if I could take working with adults. After consulting with my family, I decided to try something new and I left the classroom a better teacher and person than I was when I entered.

If you could take a look into my classroom, then fast-forward 13 years later, you'll notice that I no longer have the problems that plagued me during my first years of teaching. Instead, I've been lucky enough to stay in education and find a niche throughout all the madness. I wish 13 years ago I knew what I knew now. However, time was my teacher and it allowed me to grow not only as a professional but as a person.

As I look back at my education career, I'm thankful for all of my learning opportunities because it's allowed me to help new teachers who are struggling now. Instead of giving them solutions that will probably never work in their class, I'm able to give them tried-and-true practices that helped me survive.

My hope is that you read this book and on Monday morning, you can enter your classroom without fear, anxiety, or uneasiness.

Afterword

By Rhonda Black

Behind the Desk shares with us Franchesca Lane Warren's experiences that hundreds of thousands of first-year teachers have every year. Her evolution into one of the most well-respected and revered English teachers at Middle College High School, one of the Top 5% Reward School in the state of Tennessee within the Shelby County Schools system, lets us know that if a teacher perseveres despite the initial challenges, there is a calm after the storm. Many first-year teachers can learn from her journey.

Although barriers to success exist, there is also a plethora of resources today that were not available back when many teachers first began. In the era of President Barak Obama's education plan with a strong emphasis on teacher effectiveness, there are new teacher centers, mentoring programs, online support networks, district collaborative, and ongoing assistance through the non-tenured years that are accessible to beginning teachers. Our nation, our states and our school districts can only benefit from retaining teachers in our profession.

In addition to getting started, Warren strongly suggests that new teachers be present and professional in all growth and development activities including in-service workshops, seminars, conferences and even lunch meetings with mentors. Take the time to hone your craft, from lesson plan development to creating an engaging learning environment and designing your brand early so that you experience not just success but longevity in the profession. The days of 20- and 30-year teaching careers are no longer. Coaching and leadership opportunities are available for teachers who excel in the classroom and have talent where they can share their knowledge, skills and abilities with teacher colleagues and serve their schools and districts on a larger scale.

So as the first year of teaching can be tough, those who are committed to excelling in the profession should be even tougher. Utilize the resources available. Have a vision for your career—especially if you have the ambition to move beyond the classroom. But most importantly, be dedicated to your work, your students, and your school. Take the time to learn all the intricate details of what is now your professional career.

__Rhonda Black__ is a 20 year veteran teacher and assistant principal in Shelby County Schools located in Memphis, Tennessee. She is due to complete her Ed.D. degree later this spring from Union University in Germantown, Tennessee. Her areas of expertise are small learning communities, high school to college preparatory programs and teacher-leader effectiveness.

About the Author

Franchesca Warren is the creator of The Educator's Room, a platform to share tools and resources educators can use to empower them in the classroom. After working in several inner-city high schools across the country for over 10 years, she recognized that the true experts in education (teachers) were largely being ignored. She created the site to give teachers an outlet and since 2012, thousands of educators visit her site daily.

Within her time in education, Franchesca has taught every grade level and almost every ELA course in high school ranging from struggling readers to Advanced Placement students. In addition, she has held several leadership positions such as department chairperson, grade level team leader, curriculum writer, workshop presenter and new teacher mentor. These varied experiences has given her a unique perspective on how to improve schools—let effective teachers teach and help struggling teachers by empowering them to become experts in their respective fields. She holds steadfast to the belief that if you give teachers the tools to be successful you will not only increase teacher investment but you empower them to become instructional leaders. In 2012 she held steadfast to this belief by writing (and publishing through her company, The Educator's Room) her first educational book, *Keep the Fire Burning: Avoiding Teacher Burnout*.

An English teacher, writer, consultant, wife, and mom to three kids, Franchesca stays committed to being an agent of change. She regularly mentors several teachers from across the nation on everything from lesson planning to creating personal professional development plans. Throughout her career in education, she's been named Teacher of the Year and a Difference Maker by her colleagues. In addition, she's been featured on Fox 5 News Atlanta, Fox 13 Memphis, The Jennifer Keitt Show, The Huffington Post and several other media outlets.

A proud member of Alpha Kappa Alpha Sorority, Incorporated, Franchesca loves to volunteer in helping young girls realize their value in her community. In her spare time, you can find her running an occasional half-marathon and enjoying life with her three kids and husband in the metro Atlanta area. She lives by the motto, "Success is failure turned inside out."

Contact: Info@TheEducatorsRoom.com

Twitter: @TheEducatorsRoom

Facebook: www.Facebook.com/TheEducatorsRoom